INTERP...

AND

a beginner's guide

KRISTYNA ARCARTI

ISBN 0 340 688270

First published 1997
Impression number 10 9 8   7 6   5 4   3 2   1
Year   2000 1999 1998 1997

Typeset by Transet Limited, Coventry, England.
Printed in Great Britain for Hodder & Stoughton Educational, a division of Hodder
Headline plc, 338 Euston Road, London NW1 3BH by Cox and Wyman Limited,
Reading, Berks.

CONTENTS

INTRODUCTION   1

Chapter 1   THINKING OF SIGNS AND
SYMBOLS   3

What is a symbol?   5
Symbols we recognise easily   6
Learning about ourselves   7
Types of signs and symbols   7
Sigils, heiroglyphs, omens and codes   8

Chapter 2   HISTORICAL ROOTS OF
SYMBOLS AND SIGNS   14

Ancient animal symbolism   15
Animals of today   23
The formation of letters and scripts   33
Uses for symbols in our history   35
The formation of codes   36

Chapter 3   GEOMETRIC SYMBOLS
AND SIGNS   38

Other forms of symbol   46

Chapter 4   Combination symbols, astrology and the planets   69

Astrological symbolism   76

Chapter 5   Common symbols and their meanings   96

Chapter 6   Thinking of meditation   116

Relaxation   116
Using symbols   118
Using a mandala for meditation   120
Taking a mental Journey   121
After a meditation   126

Chapter 7   Looking at doodles   127

The position and form of doodles   128
Construction, signatures and colour   129
Looking at the symbolism   130
Looking back, and towards the future   135

Further reading   137

INTRODUCTION

This is a book about signs and symbols, not just about the obvious things these depict but also about the hidden or covert meanings. I must emphasise at the outset that there are literally thousands of symbols we could discuss, but in this book we will be able to cover only a few of these. It is hoped that this book will spark off readers' initial interest in symbolism, and will then be a stepping stone to their further research.

What though do we mean when we talk about a sign, or a symbol? Are we thinking in terms of a code, like the Morse code? Are we thinking a little more personally, like a cryptic phrase or pet name which you might use, which would only be understood by those who were close to you and identified with your 'symbol'? During the course of this book, we are going to take a look at various forms of signs and symbols, some of which may be quite familiar to us already, and unearth their hidden meanings. To understand more clearly, perhaps you should start to think of symbols and signs as a from of shorthand, itself a form of symbolism. Only those trained to use it and read it have the key. We can respond to symbols as they are, or learn more about their secrets.

It is fair to say that some signs, symbols or codes will have a personal meaning for some readers. Dreams can have a personal significance to the dreamer, for example, but other symbols and signs do have historical roots and as such a less personal and more global meaning, although it should be noted that not all civilisations or nationalities will agree with the symbolic meaning attached by others to various objects, animals, pictures or forms.

1

We will also look at various accepted meanings of signs and symbols, but it should always be remembered that the symbols involved in dreamwork often have personal meanings. Accordingly, dreams and the symbolism hidden within them are better left to books specifically written on that subject.

Psychologists for many years have dealt with signs, symbols, codes, etc. when trying to understand the minds of their patients, and we will discuss various psychiatrists' viewpoints on symbols as we progress. Most symbolism dealt with by the conscious mind concerns simple things, such as letters, numbers and obvious picture images, and it is said that the conscious mind is able to retain only around seven pieces of information at any one time. The subconscious, on the other hand, the part which deals in symbols and signs, is limitless, and it is this part of the mind which brings about dreams, themselves often symbolic. In addition, long-term memory is felt to be stored within the unconscious part of the mind. As a result of the work done especially by people like Carl Jung, the psychiatrist, much information on the subconscious meaning of signs and symbols is now available to us.

In this book, we will be looking at signs, symbols, codes, patterns, images and letters known perhaps to the conscious mind, but understood at a deeper, more unconscious level, some of these symbols having roots way back in human history. There is a strong need, especially at this point in our development as a race, for us to find our true selves, our individuality and our identity. Maybe learning a little more about our subconscious and about signs and symbols will help us all towards this end.

CHAPTER 1

THINKING OF SIGNS
AND SYMBOLS

When you start thinking about symbols, you realise that we are surrounded by them all the time. Take a look at electrical equipment – the washing machine, for example. There are symbols on the dials. We get to know the meaning of these symbols, as they correspond to the symbols on the clothing we wear. Most companies have logos – logos are symbols. Sometimes, companies change their logos, update them, feeling that the initial impact of the logo has diminished, needing to recreate a fresh interest in the product, so some symbols lose their power and disappear. We all have names. Names are also symbols. Countries have symbols – the eagle is the symbol of the United States; the bulldog is essentially symbolic of Britain, and so on. Gold and silver metals have symbols known as hallmarks, telling the initiated where the object was made and when, and other details. Looking at paper itself, you can often see a symbol in paper, called a watermark.

In the Middle Ages, tradesmen actively sought to create their own symbols to etch upon their property or with which to brand their cattle or other animals, in order to show the ownership. Even in early times, marks were chalked, painted or carved on to property, including houses, to show to others that they were owned by a particular person. From this, carpenters, stonemasons, smiths, barrel makers and many other such tradespeople actively created their own symbols, often using ideas borrowed from other sources and then personalised.

Religious symbolism is a vast subject. Many people who follow the teachings of Christendom will wear a cross or crucifix as a symbol of their religious belief. Other religions have similar symbols – the Hindus, for example, have a ceremony designed for boys between the ages of eight and twelve, where what is known as The Sacred Thread is given and worn around the body. Sometimes after the ceremony, Hindus will wear the thread around their wrist rather than around their bodies, but it is still a symbol of their commitment to the Hindu faith.

We actively use symbols every day. Many people, when talking on the telephone, for example, will doodle on a piece of paper. I mostly doodle in straight lines, making hexagonal shapes or stars (signifying idealism), but when I am in a business frame of mind, I invariably draw three-dimensional doodles (showing that I am organised and ambitious). These doodles are themselves symbols or signs, and can often tell much about our mental state at the time. They are really messages from our subconscious, in much the same way as are dream symbols, which link our subconscious minds with our fears and anxieties.

The esoteric arts contain many signs and symbols, some of which correspond to various everyday items. The minor arcana of the tarot, for example, contains as its four suits, swords, cups, coins and batons. Most of us will be able to picture these things immediately. Swords, although not in use today, are known to us through paintings, film and television. Cups and coins are everyday items to us all. Batons, also sometimes known as wands or staves, are again things which were probably more prominent in the past, but just think of a walking stick, and you can picture a baton or stave. Bible students may already have thought of the staff of Moses, which was a symbol of his power. Conversely, readers with a musical leaning may have pictured a conductor's baton. Wands will probably be familiar from fairy stories, or magazines. We think we know what all these objects are, but do we know or understand their hidden meanings? We acknowledge their meaning on a conscious level, but perhaps do not acknowledge so readily their meaning at an unconscious level. Symbolism is a fundamental part of all esoteric practices, and we will discuss these as we progress. Readers who are familiar with runes will be aware of the symbolism that each rune holds. Likewise, students of the Ogham script will know of its

symbolism and hidden meanings, and students of I Ching have studied the pattern of various lines, both broken and unbroken, that bring about hexagrams which themselves have meanings. Many of the esoteric art forms link together through their symbols and signs, many link to numbers and numerology, and we will discover many universal esoteric connections later in this book.

What is a symbol?

Symbols cover many things. Illustrations or pictures can be symbolic, and dreams can also be symbolic. There are various heraldic symbols, such as crowns, helmets, chains, etc., and there are also symbols which are more commonplace. such as road signs. We see for example, a sign depicting two elderly or bent figures, and immediately we recognise the need to slow down because there may be elderly or infirm people crossing the road. We learn to recognise symbols as we grow up. However, there is much more to symbols than merely thinking in terms of road signs and heraldic symbols.

This written page is made up of symbols, not just the letters, but also the punctuation. The full stop, for example, conveys the message that the sentence is ended, but if you think of the full stop as a dot, we have a very simple mark with a symbolic meaning quite different from ending. Triangles and circles are also basic symbols. We are surrounded by circles – the Earth is circular, as are all the planets. It is said that King Arthur had a round table as well as twelve knights (representative of the twelve signs of the zodiac), paganism has a Sacred Circle, American Indians have a Medicine Wheel, fairies are supposed to make fairy circles, standing stones are often found in circles, called cromlech (Stonehenge is a good example of this: the stones are themselves a symbol), we have interlinked circles as the symbol of the Olympic movement, and so on.

Symbols we recognise easily

Let's look at some symbols which most of us will recognise. Irrespective of whether we are looking at Egyptian hieroglyphs, at runic words or sigils, at signs, codes or pictures, various messages are conveyed. Some of these are universal, others more personal. Zodiac signs, for example, are a form of symbolism. Each sign of the zodiac will have an illustration attached to it as well as a name. Let's take Aries, as an example. Those readers who know about zodiac signs will already be thinking 'Aries, The Ram', and have formed a mental picture of a ram, and continue perhaps to think about the characteristics of Aries, or of Aries people they know.

Likewise, those who are familiar with Chinese horoscopes will be aware of the signs belonging to the various Chinese years, and

picture the animal symbols involved. We are, therefore, already thinking of the meaning behind the symbols. There are, however, many other symbols and signs, which we will discuss and learn about during the course of this book, which although familiar to us, may not immediately convey a message.

Learning about ourselves

The aim behind this book is to discuss and isolate various signs by looking at their roots and the differing interpretations various civilisations placed upon them. Having become familiar with the meaning and origin of these things, we can then take a leap forward into our modern times and see the relevance they have on our lives now, and how they link with various esoteric traditions. It will not be possible to look at each and every symbol and sign known to humans, as these are varied and extensive enough to justify an encyclopedia. Within the space that we have available to use, we will focus on the main elements involved, to generate an initial interest which you may like to take further. We will see how various ancient symbols have their place in our modern world, and how many times they are still worn as amulets of protection and power. The Egyptian ankh is one such symbol still widely used today.

Types of signs and symbols

Broadly speaking, symbols can be divided into three major categories:

- geometric or abstract shapes
- an object or a picture
- energy which is given a form in order for it to be better understood.

All these things can and do affect our subconscious minds. Once we understand these more clearly, our self-awareness will increase. This achieved, we can only move forwards.

In this book, we will be concentrating on the first two categories we have identified – the geometric signs and symbols and the object signs and symbols, although in our section on meditation, we will briefly touch upon picture symbolism. We will only be able to scratch the surface of each symbol's meanings, and I would reiterate that further study is recommended – try looking through the list of further reading at the end of this book.

Sigils, heiroglyphs, omens and codes

It is fair to say that words can often mean different things to different people. Let's start by taking the word 'sign'. If we were talking about signs on their own, some people would think in terms of proverbs – 'Red sky at night, shepherd's delight', or even in terms of omens, which we will discuss as we progress. Other people, especially those who drive for a living, might start thinking in terms of road traffic signs. Those who are interested in prophecies or omens, looking on these as 'signs', could point to various books and writers who tell of signs of approaching world changes – Nostradamus, for example. Bible students might even think of 2 Timothy: 3 where there are various signs listed as being indicative of 'the last days'. Still other people would think perhaps of sign language used to help people with a hearing impairment to understand what is being said. Yet again, other people would start to think in terms of something written – a cross at the end of a letter as a sign of love perhaps, or the codes that some people during wartime used – SWALK, for example, meaning 'Sealed with a loving kiss', giving a sign of the love of the sender for the receiver. Some of the written signs are also symbols or heiroglyphs.

Sigils

A sigil is a word or image formed out of a series of symbols, and is something with which most students of runes will be familiar. Runes themselves are signs, glyphs or symbols, and the most common meaning of the word sigil is 'runeword' – a word made up using the runic symbols, although sigils can be formed out of more personalised symbolism. We will talk about runes in a little more detail at a later stage, and there is a book in this series devoted to the study of runes and runic symbolism (see Further Reading). As with most signs and symbols, sigils are representative of unconscious images or even intentions and desires. Again, as with most signs and symbols, the actual meaning of the sigil might not immediately be obvious without some further thought.

Those readers who are familiar with the works of Austin Osman Spare will also be aware of the word sigil. Spare, who had an acute interest in psychology, and was associated both with Aleister Crowley and with Gerald Gardner, was also well known nationally for his award for mathematics and as being the youngest ever exhibitor at the National Gallery. Spare believed that sigils carried a 'power', a concept with which some readers, especially those new to the esoteric arts, may not feel comfortable.

In a later chapter, we will look at the theories behind the creation of sigils and the power that these hold, in much the same way as the power of amulets. We will also see how you may create your own sigil.

Heiroglyphs

If, like me, you have an interest in ancient Egypt, you may have learnt a little about heiroglyphs.

This ancient form of Egyptian writing was normally picture signs, and it is thought that these were first used in Egypt as long as 70,000 years ago. Used for many purposes, religious, artistic and state, the writing of heiroglyphs seems to have carried on uninterrupted until the time of Jesus Christ, after which is slowly fell into disuse, eventually to disappear around the fifth century CE.

As with the Ogham script and many other ancient forms of writing or sign, heiroglyphs were normally cut into wood or stone, or subsequently they became written on papyrus, a form of reed paper, or on flakes of white limestone. Some examples of heiroglyphs written on papyrus still exist, the Great Papyrus of Ramose III being one of the longest discovered measuring 41 metres (135 feet), and it would seem that these normally contained advice for youngsters, or love songs, as is the case with the Harris Papyrus. Most papyri were about 43 centimetres (17 inches) in width, and it is said that in Grecian times the library at Alexandria, destroyed by a fire said to have been started deliberately, contained nearly half a million papyrus rolls.

The Egyptians used heiroglyphs in many forms and in many places, not only on the walls of tombs. They kept their papyrus rolls in clay jars or wrapped in leather binding secured by thongs, and these were then stored in cavities formed in walls with each jar bearing details of its contents.

To many, the meanings of the heiroglyphs remain a mystery. Experts have studied the artwork and writing. Pictures, normally painted in bright colours, have for many centuries held a fascination. It is recorded that, having conquered Egypt in 1799, Napolean Bonapart ordered a team of French scientists to investigate the temple at Karnak. Puzzled by the inscriptions carved on the walls, they failed to understand the meaning of the building, its purpose or its builder, and they could not read the name of the Pharaoh Neb-Ma at-Ra (His Lord is the Truth of Light) nor the message written on the wall, 'God is one for all Eternity'. Around the same time, a French soldier working near Rosetta struck a basalt stone with his spade, on which was a text that had been inscribed by priests of Memphis in three scripts – Greek, ancient Egyptian hieroglyphic and Demotic. This discovery was the key to the lost language of the heiroglyphs.

Subsequent work carried out by the French Egyptologist Jean François Champollion, Dr Thomas Young, a well-known British physicist, J D Akerblad, a Swedish diplomat, and others revealed much about the meaning of the heiroglyphs, and many complete sentences were able to be deciphered. The world owes a great debt of gratitude to Chapollion, as through his work, we have been able to learn 3,000 years or more of ancient Egyptian history.

Champollion, who died in 1832, managed to decipher all three inscriptions on the Rosetta stone, forging the way for much subsequent work on the Demotic script. This was, it seems, a simplified form of writing employed for business and social purposes after around 900 BCE.

More recently, books of papyri, discovered by accident by an Egyptian peasant in 1945, have given us fifty-three texts, although it is said that the peasant actually discovered in excess of one hundred, but in ignorance left them on straw next to an oven, to find that they were used by his mother for lighting her fire. Included in the fifty-three surviving papyri are The Gospel of Thomas, Gospel of Truth, Gospel of Mary, Gospel of Philip and the Gospel of the Egyptians, which are known collectively as the Gnostic Gospels or sometimes The Secret Sayings of Jesus.

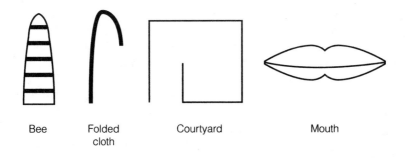

Bee   Folded cloth   Courtyard   Mouth

Those readers familiar with ancient Egypt may also be aware of the popularity of amulets, and these will be discussed in a later chapter.

Omens

Some people will automatically associate the word 'sign' with an omen. We have briefly mentioned the old adage 'Red sky at night, shepherd's delight', but many people also will view quite ordinary happenings in their lives as 'signs' or omens.

Whilst this book is not about omens or about prophecy, it is only fair to think about common omens, which many people will call signs, to enable us to be aware that omens really are totally different from signs and symbols.

Let's take the example of the black cat as a starting point. People of a superstitious nature may show concern when a black cat crosses their path, especially if it crosses from left to right, whilst others in differing parts of the world might view a black cat crossing their path as extremely lucky. Since early times, the cat has, in many civilisations, been worshipped as a god, the Egyptians associating it with the Moon and the goddesses Isis and Bast. Black, being traditionally the colour of mourning and death, when linked with the cat became something to be feared. In South America, for example, the black cat is considered to be a potent magical force, capable of causing illness and even death (again the link with the gods and heaven).

The black cat may be a symbol of magic. Most American and European people will think of the black cat as something to do with witchcraft or the devil, and many witches in legends and on film and TV will be portrayed as having a black cat as their 'familiar' – a creature capable of changing shape and form and carrying out the bidding of its owner. Similarly, in some cultures it is still believed that the cat is one of the forms into which Satan changes when he appears to mortal beings.

It is interesting to note that the cat to the ancient Egyptians was considered to be a sacred animal, representative of the Moon, possibly because its eyes dilate and contract, in much the same way as the Moon waxes and wanes. Such omens normally have as their roots the superstitions of an earlier civilisation, and such beliefs often carry on through to modern times by tradition, rather than by anything more logical or explainable. In times gone by, for example,

medieval people believed that frogs were able to cure cataracts, if you managed to catch one and spit into its mouth and mutter a magical phrase, and that the taking of lard and honey would cure angina. All these things have no scientific basis in our modern age, but other things of a similar nature seem to continue to find their way through the maze of science and study to be part of our lives now.

Omens really, then, are not signs in the sense which we are discussing here, neither are superstitions nor ancient traditions, although prophecies will continue to interest and intrigue the human mind because of our inherent desire to know and understand what the future holds.

Codes

If you are familiar with computer technology, you may be familiar with e-mail, so will already be aware that a full stop which normally ends a sentence takes on a different meaning and a different name (dot) when used in computer terminology. The symbol is the same. The meaning and name, however, differ.

Much the same can be said about codes which surround us every day. Many of these things are taken for granted in a certain format, but when used in a different way, they take on a new meaning. Let's look, for example, at braille. For those who are not familiar with this word, braille is a form of writing for the visually impaired, made up of raised dots which, when decoded, will form words. To those people who cannot read it, a page of braille will mean very little. However, to someone who has studied braille, a page of such dots and marks will mean a story, a poem, an article or whatever. To a sighted person, that dot can mean a full stop at the end of a sentence, or it can have hidden innuendos, as in the case of 'Well you know all about her, don't you ….'.

Within the world of symbols and codes, however, the dot or full stop can mean a lot more, and we uncover these meanings later in this book. However, before we can do this, we should take a look at the historical roots of various symbols and signs.

hISTORICAL ROOTS OF SYMBOLS AND SIGNS

Although only a little way into our journey of discovery of the meaning of various signs and symbols, we can appreciate that we are surrounded by such things all the time. It is not surprising, therefore, to realise that humankind has always been surrounded by signs and symbols; sometimes they have a practical use and sometimes a more esoteric or magical purpose.

Symbols convey a message which makes you think. They belong in every avenue of life, and have always played a huge part in religious matters, in ceremonies, artwork and tradition. Most religions have common elements, even if the roots are somewhat different.

If you have an interest in psychology, you will know that symbols often carry a message to us somewhere deep within. They react with our gut feelings. Being, therefore, part of the language of the unconscious, as well as the conscious mind, they also connect to various archetypal things which have a place in history.

Over the years, as traditions wane and are replaced by more current thinking, many symbols lose their original meaning and/or impact. Psychiatrist Carl Jung maintained that if symbols are not constantly renewed, they lose their dissolubility and power, and symbols which become well known may be used for commercial concerns as logos. To understand symbols and signs, we need to get to know what they are. In much the same way as, when growing up, we learn what the various symbols around us mean, it is sometimes necessary to learn about the other symbols which surround us, which perhaps we might not always notice or recognise as conveying a meaning.

Paleolithic people, whose existence revolved mainly around hunting animals, finding shelter and forming a group, etched various symbols on the walls of the caves in which they lived. Such rock carvings and paintings have subsequently given us much insight into the lifestyle of these people, and their symbolism is echoed still in various tribal paintings in Africa, although it is uncertain what some of the linear graphics meant, even though some of them resemble the characters of alphabets which came later. This is the case with some artefacts said to date from the end of the sixth century BCE, which bear inscriptions including the cross and the swastika.

Symbols were used which reflected everyday life, and it is generally accepted that the most universal symbols were stones (used as implements and as a means of sharpening tools, as well as being places thought to be the home of spirits), animals (food and clothing) and circles (looking towards the heavens one saw round objects in the sky).

As we have already identified, symbols form three distinct groups, one of which is the object or picture group. From a historical angle, it is important to look at the symbolism involved with animals, both real and mythological.

Ancient animal symbolism

Animals have always been used for symbols, even the most primitive drawings, stretching back as far as the Ice Age, seem to have included animals. Respected for their power, their speed and their strength, many animals became symbolic of gods and goddesses, and most early civilisations worshipped such figures.

Birds

Many civilisations had bird gods: birds, because they are able to soar into the heavens, were seen to have a strong connection with gods. In many ancient cultures, the Babylonian and Egyptians being just two, it was thought that the soul departed the body in the form of a bird, and birds themselves became symbolic of many things.

The dove had huge symbolical relevance, as both a Christian symbol of peace, innocence, love and the power of the Holy Spirit, and also to other groups as a symbol of the rising of the soul at death. The dove is, in fact, one of the first two birds mentioned in the Bible, and Genesis tells us that Noah sent out a dove after the flood, knowing that food would be available when the bird came back with something in its mouth. Generally, doves are symbols of devotion and innocence, and 'my dove' is sometimes used as a pet name by lovers. Two doves, especially, are considered to be a sign of married bliss, and the bird is said to be sacred to Venus, the goddess of love. Doves were also spiritual creatures to the Iroquois Indians. In Eastern religions, it is quite common to think that heaven is full of singing birds who are, in fact, the souls of the righteous. In a later chapter, we will take a look at other bird symbolism, as well as discussing the animals linked with astrology.

Combining human and animal forms

Many civilisations actively sought to combine the animal and human forms to depict their gods, and this in turn gave rise to the use of such forms as the siren, a figure usually shown as either a bird-woman or a fish-woman, common in Greek mythology. These creatures were said to entice to death the crews of ships by their singing, and thus were symbolic of temptation and feminine seduction. Similarly, the minotaur, half man and half bull, is a common mythological symbol, said to represent the monsterous side of mankind, passion and force. Likewise, the mermaid, half woman and half fish is well known, especially so since the writing of Hans Christian Andersen, but the thought of such a creature probably dates from ancient Syria, as their sea goddess Atergatis is depicted on Phoenician coins as a mermaid.

Mythological animal symbols

Animals have always held symbolic relevance, even in our modern times, and although we don't always appreciate it, we still use animals as symbols – one such animal is the Dodo, a creature now symbolic of extinction, hence the expression 'As dead as the Dodo'. Various mythological animal symbols came into prominence and disappeared, but a few remain.

Unicorn

The unicorn is a very complex symbol. It is seen in early artwork dating from Egyptian times, shown normally as being sacrificed to the Moon goddess Isis, and also in other artwork from Babylon and Assyria. Considered by most to be symbol of purity, as a Christian symbol the unicorn was often thought to be symbolic of Mary, mother of Jesus, and as such was linked with chastity and purity of action and thought. It also symbolises stability, and it is said, according to Jewish legend, that it was too big to travel in Noah's Ark, and had to be towed behind by a rope attached to its horn. Many Greek writers, however, talked of its fierce and proud nature, its power and strength, and it thus became symbolic of a violent and sometimes cruel person. Known to the Chinese many centuries before the dawning of Christianity, and given the name Ch'ilin or Ky-lin, a unicorn is said to have appeared to Confucius's mother in the sixth century shortly before his birth, and thus the unicorn became symbolic to the Chinese of the birth of a great person, and was a familiar symbol on the doors of women's homes throughout Asia, hopeful that they would produce a high ranking person or someone who would later become prominent. Thought to be fairly solitary creature, the unicorn was often used as a symbol of a monastic existence, although the Hebrews felt it to be symbolic of power and strength.

In alchemy, the unicorn is symbolic of the union of masculine and feminine principles. Astrologically the unicorn represented the Moon while the lion was the Sun (some scholars feel that the original sign for Capricorn was the unicorn, although others think it is a goat with a fish tail). The links between the Moon (darkness) and the Sun (light) led to the unicorn being associated with the fight between good and evil, light and dark and the yin/yang principle, and so consequently, the unicorn came to symbolise balance and justice. In heraldry coats-of-arms are often depicted, especially in Britain, by a lion and a unicorn supporting a shield. In fact, King Edward III used both the lion and the unicorn as an emblem at certain times, and the royal arms of Scotland in the reign of King James V showed a red lion on a golden shield, with two silver unicorn supporters. Consequently, the unicorn and the lion became two symbols for Britain.

Whilst most people would suggest that the unicorn is a mythical creature, it is said that Julius Caesar actually saw a unicorn in Germany. Although its origin is uncertain, its usage in symbolism, especially religious symbolism is well recorded. Like the phoenix and the dragon, also ancient symbols, the unicorn's use in symbolism gradually dwindled, although it still appears in fables and stories.

With the dawning interest in anything termed 'New Age', the unicorn symbol has undergone a revival, becoming the symbol for the Age of Aquarius. The single horn growing from the centre of the unicorn's forehead symbolises the psychic third eye, and reflects the growing interest in anything esoteric.

Dragon

The dragon is a universally recognised symbol, again somewhat complex, whose name would appear to come from the Greek word *derkein*, meaning 'seeing'. Thus the animal is given the attribute of having extraordinary eyesight. It is particularly popular still in China, where it forms part of the processions at the commencement of the Chinese New Year, and is thought to be a symbol of authority, bringing long life and happiness. As students of Chinese astrology will be aware, the dragon forms one of the twelve animals of the zodiac, being symbolic of the highest spiritual power. Dragons in China and the Far West are respected creatures, who can take on a

variety of guises. Chinese dragons are basically grouped into five separate categories – heavenly or imperial, celestial, spiritual, earthly and subterranean. They are further divided by colour – red and black dragons are considered ferocious and evil, whilst blue dragons symbolise fertility and the coming of the spring, and white dragons are symbolic of power, energy and healing.

Linked closely to snakes, serpents and the ouroboros (a Gnostic dragon/snake creature biting its tail), dragons have appeared in various forms in myths and legends from around 5000 BCE. There are stories of dragons in ancient Babylon and Assyria, and the dragon is also a symbol in parts of Africa, India and amongst the early Americans. It features in Greek and Roman myth, but its first appearance in classical mythology links it with the Typhon, a creature in Greek myth associated with hurricanes and volcanoes. One of the most famous of mythological dragons from the Greek period is Ladon, who guarded the apples of the Hesperides. The earliest symbolical use for the dragon appears in Babylonian legends, where it was used to represent the struggle between good and evil, light and dark, day and night, much the same as the unicorn.

The Greek writer Artemidorus then linked it with guardianship, especially of wealth, and during the Middle Ages, many believed that the dragon lived beneath the surface of the Earth, and could, at any time, find itself in the world, where it would wreak havok. Thus the dragon became symbolic of the power of evil, lurking just beneath the surface in humankind itself, and our need to protect ourselves against its forces. Likewise, its connection with wealth lead to its usage as the 'beast of materialism' and our need to protect ourselves from greed and averice.

There are literally hundreds of stories about dragons in differing countries. England, especially, has many such stories. In these tales, dragons are usually at least 6 metres (20 feet) in length, with scales and a tail, and whilst some have wings, others do not. Dragons have featured as emblems within coats-of-arms for many centuries, and were thought to be symbolic of a terrible power. If you know of the story of St George you will also be aware that the dragon represents something which should be slayed because of its wickedness. There are thirteen mentions in the Bible of the dragon, all conveying the idea of the devil and Satan, and as such being something to be subdued and then destroyed, something to fight against.

The story of George and the Dragon could merely be an updating of an earlier Greek myth, where Perseus rescued Andromeda from a sea serpent sent by Neptune, but other stories suggest that George was not British anyway, but a Greek knight who killed a dragon in Libya. It seems the monster had attacked the town of Silene and its poisonous breath had killed everyone who inhaled it. Various sacrifices failed to save the situation, until the princess, sent by her father the king, went outside the city walls as a tribute to the dragon. She was met by George, who just happened to be passing. He took out his silver crucifix and pinned the dragon to the ground with his lance. As a result, the knight became famous amongst the Crusaders, and King Edward III adopted him in 1415 as the patron saint of England after the English victory at Agincourt.

Dragons, however, also connect with St Michael who, in medieval times, was known by the title 'Michael the Dragon Slayer'. In its form as the ouroboros, which often has several meanings depending on the actual illustration given, the dragon is often symbolic of anything relating to the passing of time. To Jung, the dragon was representative of the mother figure, although he did acknowledge that it could be seen to represent evil. In fact, to people in many differing countries the dragon has always conveyed an idea of fertility, and the heralding of the spring. To the early British, the dragon was often used as an ensign during periods of war, as was the case with King Arthur's father, Uther Pendragon, and became associated with feelings of victory, whilst to the Greeks and Romans, the dragon was a creature of wisdom, and with its keen eyesight was often found guarding the entrance to temples. A symbol of elemental power, to pagans the dragon is symbolic of the Cailleach who holds the power of winter over Brigit's lamb, symbolic of spring.

Phoenix

The phoenix, another mythical creature which features in many

cultures, is symbolic of destruction and re-creation, and thus can be linked to both the Sun and the Moon. Its origin is unknown, but it seems to come from ancient Egypt, where it was called *bennu*, the 'sun bird', emblematic of the Sun god Ra, and linked to Osiris as it was said to contain his soul. Legends tell that the phoenix lived to over 1,000 years of age, was larger than an eagle, and lived in a wooded area, linked to paradise. When it reached the age of 1,000 it flew to Arabia, picking up various perfumes as it travelled, from whence it flew to Phoenicia to make its nest. At dawn, it sang, its voice being so beautiful that it awakened the Sun god, and sparks were sent from his halo which ignited the nest. As the bird was consumed by the fire within the nest, a new bird arose, which flew towards the Sun, followed by other birds who had picked up its perfume, and then returned to the wooded area for another 1,000 years. As a result, the phoenix became symbolic of resurrection and the triumph of life over death, of renewal and regeneration. Christendom saw the attributes of this phoenix as Christ-like, and used it as a symbol of the resurrection which often features on early Christian tombs and on the coins of early Christian emperors. The Chinese consider the phoenix to be emperor of the birds, and a symbol of the Sun, and it is used in talismans to this effect in both China and Japan. This mythical bird was thought to have a long life, and to the Chinese it is often worn as an amulet to promote happiness, especially in marriage, fidelity, benevolence and a long life. In Japan, it is a talisman for uprightness, justice and honesty.

Griffin

Various animal symbols seeking to combine the attributes of differing species were historically used as symbols, and these include the griffin, an animal which appears to be half eagle and half lion, which was felt to guard the road leading to salvation. As such it was often depicted standing alongside the Tree of Life. Symbolising the relationship between the mystical and the material, and also connected with vigilance and persistence, the griffin was a very popular symbol during the Middle Ages, and in early Christian art was often used to represent both the Messiah and the antichrist.

Chimera

Another such animal was the chimera, an animal mentioned by Homer as a fire-breathing monster, part lion, part goat and part snake. Symbolically, this animal represents the divine powers of creation, destruction and conservation, and is found linked to storms and winds.

The Giants amongst us

In addition to animals whose existence we can no longer prove, we also have, in history, the stories of the giant, one of the most ancient symbols used by early civilisations. Giants sometimes were evil in intent and sometimes depicted as good, those who protected others.

However, there are stories of the giant being slain, and as such its height, strength and aggression are paralleled by the feeling that the giant can be beaten. Consequently, the giant often became the symbol for humankind itself, in permanent rebellion, but able to be subdued. Symbolic of strength and stature, the giant was considered by Jung to be merely a depiction of the father figure, seen from the eyes of his children, and thus endowed with the element of protection. Stories of giants are many, and there are mentions of them in the Bible, not only Goliath, who stood nearly 3 metres (9 feet 6 inches), but also Og, king of Bashan who stood over 4 metres (13 feet) and had a width of nearly 2 metres (6 feet). In addition, in Genesis, the Bible tells of the Nephilim, people who perished in the flood, who were also of extraordinary size, the product of the mating of angels and women, and it is interesting that sometimes, especially in early Christian artwork, the devil is portrayed as a giant. Most civilisations have their giants – Hercules, Gargantua (from where we get the word gargantuan, meaning huge), Titan and others.

The Green Man

Another popular symbol of ancient Nature worshippers was The Green Man. The figure of the Green Man is obviously a masculine face, sometimes quite beautiful and sometimes really grotesque,

which appears to be peering through leaves and foliage which sometimes take the form of a beard or even of horns. Early Greek and Roman gods were often thus portrayed (Silvanus and Baccus being just two), and there are similar figures in India, ancient Babylon and Islamic artwork.

A common embellishment in ancient churches and cathedrals, used as a decoration on bibles and other Christian artwork, the Green Man can also be found on the tomb of Pope Julius II in Rome, but his name is now familiar as a name for a public house. The Green Man was probably one of the early pagan gods, symbolic of the life-force and spirit of Nature, a divine King of the May, and he is connected with regeneration, rebirth and fertility and with things of the Earth. Said by students of witchcraft to have the ability when used in spellworking to bring love back into your life, his appearance on the outside of churches was said to have been used to frighten away the devil and his demons, but it is well documented that the early Christians actively encouraged the usage of pagan symbolism in an attempt to incorporate as many new believers as possible into the faith. Old traditional teachings were not abandoned, but simply adapted to suit the designs of the time.

Seen in modern times as part and parcel of the Morris dancing tradition, and also associated with various customs when he is given the name of Jack in the Green, his earliest appearance in artwork seems to be on a tomb in France dating back to 400 BCE.

Animals of today

There are many animals known to us today which have a historical use in symbolism, and whilst we are not able to look at every such animal, we will concentrate our energies on looking at a sample few. Animals associated with astrology will be discussed in a later chapter.

Snake

The snake, or serpent, was well known to Christians as being the animal form which Satan took in the Garden of Eden. The Bible account in Genesis states that it was the serpent or snake which, through its lies and deceit, persuaded Eve to eat from the tree from which God had expressly forbidden them to eat, as a result of which sin was born, so the snake became symbolic of deceit and disobedience. In fact, often the biblical Tree of Life is depicted as having around it a coiled snake, and thus has become symbolic of the evil around us at all times. To the Hebrews, especially, the snake or serpent is symbolic of evil and the souls of those who live in permanent hell.

The snake features in most cultures, but its symbolic meaning and connections differ, and as such it has become a symbol of the union of opposites, and also a phallic symbol. Sometimes it is considered to be masculine in principle, other times feminine, and as a symbol it is often interchangeable with the dragon. Its forked tongue has led it to be symbolic to many of deceit and being 'sharp tongued'. Connected to water, to the Japanese thunder god, Susanoo, and to the Celtic god Cernunnos, to students of ley lines or spirit tracks the snake image is symbolic of the flow of currents of energy through the Earth. To the Chinese, it is something favourable, forms one of the twelve animals of the Chinese astrology system, and symbolises energy and movement. It can be seen by most groups to be something both good and evil, whilst its abilities to strangle its prey lead it to be connected with strength. This latter thought was particularly significant to the Mayans. In Japanese and Chinese myth, snake-women are quite common. Snakes were also thought by the Indians to be guardians of wealth and treasure, and they thought that a man who died without leaving a son and heir would return to the Earth as a snake to guard his wealth. The Naga or Nagini hooded snakes which are often depicted as having seven heads, are said to guard Buddha and bring rain.

To pagan Britain, the snake was also considered a good symbol, representing wisdom, fertility and energy, and as a result it became a custom in early Christianity to call all pagans 'serpents'. In fact, many ancient gods and goddesses are depicted with coiled snakes about their person. Generally considered to represent eternity, regeneration and renewal of life (by the way in which it sheds its

skin) and of power, the snake as an amulet became connected to thoughts of long life, vitality and good health.

The Greek god Asclepius, famous for his healing powers, is closely connected with snakes, but worship of snake gods and goddesses was not confined only to Europe and the Middle East, but also appears in various Indian tales, especially in the Hindu stories, where Hindu god Krishna is said to have battled with the serpent gods who were far older than his worship. Considered by the ancient Greeks to be symbolic of a dead hero or god, snakes were also symbolic of protection. The heiroglyphics of the ancient Egyptians often feature snakes and serpents, symbolic of new beginnings, whilst to others it is considered to be representative of the healing process. Egyptian stories tell us that Set, who murdered Horus's father Osiris, could change into a snake, and it is interesting to note the biblical connection with the changing of the staff or stave into a snake at the court of the Egyptians, which we have already mentioned. To the Egyptians the snake was considered both good and bad. There were good snake goddesses Buto and Edjo, who were protectors, but Apep and Nek were evil, and had to be slain by Ra in cat form. Likewise, in Norse mythology, the snake Jorgumgander, which lives in Midgard, is said to encircle the Earth or conversely wait at the bottom of the sea for the end of the world to come.

Snakes, however, representative of hidden potential, were things to be treated with respect, and Isis and Nepthys both take snake form on the brow of the Sun god as the sacred Uraeus. To the Indians, the snake is connected with immortality, and with the element of Water, whilst to other cultures, it is considered to be a symbol of wisdom. To psychologists, especially students of Freud, however, the snake is a phallic symbol which represents the sperm and the ovum. Possibly this latter thought comes from Gnostic teachings, where the image of the Orphic Egg was of a serpent, representative of the male principle, wrapped three and a half times around the egg, representative of the female principle.

The Gnostic ouroboros can also be representative of both dark and light, much as the Chinese yin/yang symbol conveys a similar meaning – a combination not only of light and dark, but also of positive and negative, male and female, good and bad, in fact any opposing factors.

If you are familiar with yoga, you will know that the snake is often used to symbolise the kundalini, coiled up at the lower end of the spinal column, awaiting release, which will lead to ultimate enlightenment as it travels through the various chakra centres. The word kundalini actually means 'fire snake', and yogic teachers can show students how to awake this coiled serpent by various techniques (see *Chakras for Beginners* in this series).

LAMB

Another animal with strong religious connections is the lamb. Biblical links are many: the lamb is very common in the Near East, and lambs were sacrificed regularly in ancient Israel. Biblically, lambs become symbolic of meekness, obedience and the need for protection, and also as a symbol of purity, innocence and sacrifice. Jesus is called the lamb by John the Baptiser, and subsequently the lamb is mentioned twenty-eight times in Revelation. The lamb has thus become a symbol of the Saviour, and of a triumph of life over death. Consequently the lamb features strongly in church artwork, carvings and sculptures, where Jesus can be shown carrying the lamb (caring for his flock). Ancient amulets showing a lamb carrying a cross and flag can still be seen, and it is felt by many that carrying this 'Agnus Dei' will protect the wearer from ill fortune. Sheep and shepherds feature strongly in the Bible.

DOG

The dog is generally considered symbolic of faithfulness, loyalty and compassion, and artwork from the Middle Ages and later times has sought to depict this by placing dogs at the feet of women, both in portraits and in other artwork. As such, the dog is considered to be a feminine symbol. A recently discovered dog cemetery from the Persian period at Ashkelon suggests that the people of the time viewed the dog in quite a positive way, and many of the ancient gods were seen to have dogs as constant companions. In fact, the god of healing Asclepius, was normally depicted with his dog, leading the dog to be considered as having a possible healing quality. This may well be true, as most people familiar with therapeutic touch will tell how stroking a dog can lower blood pressure and lead to a feeling of well-being. However, in biblical times, the dog was considered to be unclean, a scavenger and something to be shunned, and dogs are mentioned quite negatively in most cases in the Bible, linked to sorcerers, idolators and fornicators. In some countries, to call a person 'a dog' is still a symbol of the deepest contempt. In Zoroastrianism, however, the dog is sacred, and is linked with vigilance, fidelity and kindness. In fact, dogs are treated with the greatest respect and feature in several of the Zoroastrain traditions.

To many, dogs are symbolic of friendship, and students of Chinese astrology will know that it is another one of the animals of Chinese astrology, where it signifies warmth, love, duty and loyalty. The dog is also symbolic of the protector – the dog which guards the house or the sheep, whilst to many ancient civilisations, the dog was considered to be the animal which accompanied the dead on their journey to another world. Ancient records tell us that, in Egypt, it was considered necessary to completely shave one's body of hair upon the death of a dog.

FROG

The frog again has several symbolic meanings. Symbolic to many as a link between the elements of Water and Earth, to the ancient Egyptians, the frog was representative of health and long life, linked with Herit or Heqt, the goddess who assisted Isis in her resurrection of Osiris, often depicted as having the head of a frog, and who was considered to be the goddess who watched over conception and birth. Known also as the midwife goddess, her protection promised fine healthy children, and as such the use of the frog amulet was considered essential to those who wished to have a successful pregnancy and delivery. The frog was also used as an amulet considered to symbolise transformation and resurrection, and the symbol is often found on the walls of burial chambers. Egyptians who subsequently embraced Christianity continued to use the frog to symbolise new births and the resurrection, whilst the Greeks, Turks and Italians felt that the frog was symbolic of good health. To the ancient Romans, the frog was the symbol of Aphrodite, the goddess of love, and as such became a talisman used by lovers to promote love, faithfulness, fertility and a happy relationship. The Bible tells us that a plague of frogs was sent to Egypt, in order to bring into disrepute the worship of frog gods and goddesses.

Lion

The Lion is again heavily used in symbolism, especially in heraldry. In Egypt, it was thought that the lion patrolled the banks of the Nile, supervising the annual floods, and as such it was highly respected. To many ancient civilisations, the lion linked with the Sun, and eventually it found its way into Christian symbolism, being linked with St Mark, and thence into heraldry. Uses for the lion are many and varied. History students of English history will know that King Richard became known as Richard the Lionheart, because of his courage and leadership, whilst Bible students will know that David and Samson both killed lions, and that Daniel was thrown into the lion's den. Lions were engraved in the temples of many ancient civilisations, and it is recorded that twelve lions lined the steps of Solomon's throne. In the Bible, lions are mostly symbols of courage and confidence. Courageous men are often described as 'having the heart of a lion', and the fearlessness of the lion is also linked to God's determination to protect His people at Isaiah 31:4 and 5. The lion is also symbolic of the tribes, and Jesus is said in Revelation to

be 'the lion that is of the tribe of Judah', following on from the association of Judah with a lion in Genesis 49:9. In Psalms, however, the lion is linked to wickedness, and often the roaring lion is linked to Satan. In the main, however, lions in the Bible are symbolic of courage, justice and invincibility, and are used to speak of hostility, warfare and personal enemies.

The lion is a prominent part of Western astrology, where it symbolises the zodiac sign of Leo, and connects strongly with the Sun. Thought by some to be representative of the Earth, the lion was felt by Jung to be symbolic of passion and the possible dangers of being eaten up by the unconscious mind. Generally, the lion is considered to be a symbol of strength, valour and power, and also a strongly masculine sign. Ancient Celtic gods used lion symbols and the Romans carved lions on their buildings and made statues of them. Lions have always been considered to be symbolic of power, justice and guardianship, and as such its usage within British heraldry is often thought appropriate.

CAT

The cat has always been used symbolically, and we have already made brief mention of cats and their association with omens. To the ancient Egyptians, it was considered sacred to the goddesses Isis and Bast and linked with the Moon, possibly because its pupils dilate, much as the Moon waxes and wanes, as we have already mentioned. Records tell us that, upon the death of a cat in Egypt, people were expected to shave off their eyebrows, and cats were often mummified. To the ancient Romans, the cat with its independent nature was a symbol of liberty and freedom, whilst to early Christians, the cat was considered to be one of the many forms used by Satan, and this has been sustained in various ways with the thought that black cats are the familiars of witches, and thus considered symbolic of evil and the power of darkness. In Norse tradition, the cat is linked with Freya who controls the night and who has her chariot drawn by cats. This link has lead the cat to be symbolic of love and passion, as Freya was strongly associated with these attributes.

Eagle

The eagle, as we have already identified, is presently used as the symbol of the United States. Its use as the symbol for a country is not, however, new, as it was used as such by both the ancient Babylonians and the Persians, and came to be regarded as a symbol of all the sky gods, being connected directly to Jupiter. To the Egyptians, however, the eagle symbolically represented the letter A, and as such signified the beginning, and also possibly because of this connection, it also signified the father. Records show that many armies used the eagle as their symbol, including Germany, and it is noteworthy that the emperor Charlemagne and Napoleon Bonaparte also actively used the eagle as their symbol.

Considered by early Christians to be symbolic of John the Baptiser, and being the most frequently mentioned bird in the Bible, the image is used as a symbol of authority, rank, dignity and strength, and it appeared on early Roman coins to signify power. The Romans also used it on the aquilia, the standard of the Roman army, in fact many ancient armies, including the Babylonians and Persians marched under the banner of the eagle, and it was also used as a symbol of the departing of the soul to the heavens at the funeral of Roman emperors. Other Christian analogies are that the eagle shows resurrection through baptism, and stands for the inspiration of the Gospels, and is often linked, along with the dove, to the spirit, and thus is used in many churches on lecturns. In the Bible, however, the eagle is normally used to symbolise wisdom, divine protection and swiftness. To alchemists, the eagle symbolised the liberated spirit, whilst in Hebrew tradition it is symbolic of renewal, although considered unclean by the Jews.

In the Bible in Deuteronomy 32:9–12, we can see how the eagle was used as a symbol of divine protection. In Isaiah, the eagle is compared to his spiritual strength, telling how the eagle soars higher and higher into the sky, and the eagle is also used to illustrate the belief that those who trust in God will not tire or grow weary. Often, the message of the eagle's effortless flight is liked to God's strength to lift us up spiritually and emotionally so that we can carry on. The eagle is also mentioned in Ezekiel where it is symbolic of wisdom,

using the analogy of its keen eyesight. With its ability to see far into the distance and take precautions against imminent danger, the eagle, to the Spanish, is used to symbolise someone with insight and discernment. Because of its ability to soar to great heights, ancient peoples often considered the eagle to be symbolic of the spirit of the Sun, also possibly because it was thought to have the ability to gaze directly at the Sun. The ancient Syrians certainly thought so, whilst many, especially the orientals, considered it to be a symbol of warfare, linking it to many gods of war. Eagles are swift in flight, and again the Bible uses this in Lamentations, where the Babylonian soldiers (who as we are aware used to march under the banner of the eagle) are linked to the swiftness of eagles. The Bible frequently uses the swiftness of the eagle to symbolise the speed of military forces, especially in 2 Samuel and Jeremiah.

Its use in religion is wide, being considered by St Jerome to be symbolic of the ascension and the travelling of prayer up to the heavens, and also as the symbol for the spiritual self, which can triumph over the physical. The eagle is often depicted in stories in various struggles with other animals, and is normally seen as victorious, again symbolically showing the victory of Spirit over other elements. As a result, the eagle is symbolic of fearlessness, dignity and quick perception. Like the phoenix, it was also reputed to be able to renew its plummage. Egyptian stories tell that, as part of the celebration at On-Heliopolis, the chief Sun temple of Egypt, an eagle with painted wings was burned alive with spices in a nest of palm leaves. Representative of the Sun, the palm being sacred to the great goddess his mother, the eagle rose and became new once more.

fish

The fish has many symbolic meanings, again altering from country to country, and to some people it is considered to be a phallic symbol, possibly due to the amount of eggs it lays, and thus is also symbolic of fertility. In Buddhism, the fish is symbolic of finding refuge in Buddha, Buddha himself often being referred to as Fisher of Men, a thought also found within Christianity, where the disciples were referred to as Fishers of Men. To the ancient Egyptians, the fish represented Hathor, the cow-headed goddess, who was thought to control the rising of the Nile and the irrigation of crops, and it is recorded that Egyptian kings were not allowed to eat fish. The fish was regarded by many ancient people as a symbol of abundance and a possible increase in riches and good fortune (those who owned fishing boats were often wealthy and high in status); the Chinese word for fish links with the word for abundance, and consequently, the fish is symbolic of wealth. The early Christians, possibly working from the account of the feeding of the 5,000, used the fish as a symbol of Jesus, the spiritual world and everlasting life, also explaining that the Greek word for fish (*ichthys*) used the letters of the Greek words which meant 'Jesus Christ, Son of God, Saviour'. Found carved on many early Christian catacombs, the fish became a secret sign of brotherhood especially to the early Christian martyrs, whilst those who know a little about astrology will be aware that the zodiac sign of Pisces is depicted by fish. The tradition of Catholics to eat fish on Fridays possibly stems from a similar tradition employed by various other religious groups. Isis, Ishtar and Aphrodite had, as their sacred day, Friday, and fish was then eaten in their honour.

Certain types of fish carry their own symbolism. The dolphin, for example, is generally regarded as symbolic of salvation.

TORTOISE

The tortoise is highly regarded in China, Japan and India, where is it considered to be a symbol of the universe, and called a celestial emblem. Generally felt to be symbolic of persistence (the story of the hare and the tortoise is well known), to many the tortoise is symbolic of a hard exterior protecting a softer nature inside. In Taoism, the shell, domed and bending, represents the sky, whilst the body of the animal represents the Earth, and many Eastern civilisations have artwork showing the tortoise supporting the world on its back. Due to the fact that it lives a long time, it is also symbolic of longevity (along with the crane) and also of wisdom, and is sometimes used as a talisman against evil. A common symbol for longevity in China is the linked use of the tortoise and the snake, whose union, it was thought, created the universe. Associated with fertility, especially in Africa, the tortoise is to Christians symbolic of modesty, as its habit of going back into its shell when approached was felt to connect with this attribute.

Scarab

Prominent in ancient Egypt especially, was the scarab or dung
beetle. Linked to Kheper or Khepri, a form of Sun god and also
consequently the god of resurrection, it was linked to the Sun and to
creation, not only because of its links with the gods, but also
because the beetle rolled its eggs in ox dung from east to west,
resembling the movement of the Sun across the skies, and because
it was seen to fly directly into the Sun at the hottest part of the day.
Because the beetle rolled its eggs in ox dung and buried these in the
ground for twenty-eight days, the scarab was also linked to the lunar
cycle and to the menstrual cycle. On the twenty-ninth day, the
young beetle emerged, and so it is not surprising that the scarab
became associated with rebirth and new life, and was symbolic of
strength, virility and improved health. Scarab amulets are known to
have been placed on the chest of a dead person, so that the soul
would be protected and guaranteed a new life elsewhere. Some of
these amulets were quite small, especially those used in jewellery,
whilst other scarab amulets were carved in granite and rock. As a
talisman, the scarab was used to attract good luck, guarantee good
health and give strength. Scarabs are male in principle, and,
although normally associated with the Sun, are linked to the Moon
by certain African tribes.

Further discussion of animals will be given in a later chapter when
we look especially at Chinese astrological symbolism.

The formation of Letters and scripts

As early civilisations progressed, in order to convey ideas and
speech patterns which began to emerge rather than becoming reliant
on pictures, various alphabets came to be formed. Most early forms
of such writing were made by straight lines, strokes or scores made
on wood or stone, and scripts such as runic and Ogham became

commonplace in Europe. In other lands, similar scripts emerged, again mostly using straight lines, circles or combinations of such, and it is interesting to see how various symbols, which appear to our eyes to be the same, conveyed totally different messages to peoples of differing countries. A thorough discussion of the runic script and the Ogham script is not possible here, but I would really recommend anybody who is interested in the formation of language and ancient alphabets to carry out further research on the Ogham script, which although no longer used, possibly was one of the most powerful forms, along with the Bobileth, the language of the trees.

The ancient Phoenicians provided the starting point for many languages which followed on. The Egyptian forms of hieroglyphics represented both objects, sounds, letters and powers, as did the Hebrew to some extent, which had links with magical powers and thoughts in the Qabalah, as well as linking with numbers (gematria), a study in its own right. Numerology – the use of numbers in symbolism – is worth further investigation. The books *Numerology for Beginners* and *Qabalah – a beginner's guide* in this series will provide a good starting point.

Many ancient alphabets are connected with numbers, including the Greek, and several systems which developed linked to both the Qabalah and to Pythagorus. It is thought that the Qabalistic teachings started with Abraham, and the information passed verbally from person to person, never being written down for fear that it would fall into the wrong hands. As a result, many Qabalistic symbols are still shrouded in mystery.

Taking the Hebrew alphabet as a staring point, the first letter of the Hebrew alphabet is Aleph. This is very similar to our letter A. Symbolically, this letter also carried the meaning of ox or cattle, and thus, because many people traded in such animals, it also became symbolic of wealth. As you work your way through the Hebrew alphabet, each letter conveys a similar symbolism, all connected with things which the people of early times could understand – houses, camels, doors, swords, fences, etc. Similarly, looking at ancient Greek, one can see many similarities, each alphabetical symbol also having other meanings, and it is interesting to see that

again, for the letter Alpha (A in our Western alphabet) the symbolism is of cattle, although to many this letter is symbolised by a bird.

Names

Names, as we have already seen, are themselves symbols, and it is not surprising that the Egyptians, as well as many other peoples, placed considerable importance on the name of a person. Names have always been considered to have their own meaning. Even in modern times, people still consult name books prior to the birth of children, to see whether the name carries a positive energy or not. In ancient Egypt, for example, the name Osiris meant 'he who is at the top of the steps (to evolution)'. As the Egyptians thought that the name of the dead person could live on with them in heaven, and that names were a reflection of the soul, their names were recorded, written or spoken after their death, in order that they would continue to exist. Pharoahs and other high ranking officials even carved or painted their names several times on the walls of tombs and temples. As such, graffiti is not a new concept!

Uses for symbols in our history

Alchemy, a forerunner of modern chemistry and the study of metals, also carried within it a huge symbolic and magical element, and this was again something studied deeply by the psychiatrist Jung. Using, as it does, various ancient esoteric arts, alchemy was at its peak during the Middle Ages and the Renaissance, but returned to prominence following a lecture on symbolism given by Jung in 1935. Archetypes, thoughts and predispositions towards certain patterns of behaviour which Jung felt were passed down from ancestors to the present day, also featured heavily in his work, and such energies were, he felt, often connected to pagan god symbols. Likewise, he felt that the symbol of the Grail, connected with the legend of King Arthur, was but another way of expressing our search for truth and our need to rediscover our real self.

Many magical and ancient alchemical letters were used in the preparation of talismans and used in the workings carried out in magic circles, and many preparations had to be formulated to ensure the correct and proper usage of these symbols. Subsequently, due to an amalgamation of thoughts and the creation of new systems which incorporated personal sigils, alchemical and astrological symbols and geomantic or linear symbols, new magical symbols appeared, including the Theban and Apollonian scripts, used extensively in magical workings.

The formation of codes

Following on from the growing interest in magical symbols, during the Middle Ages many secret societies, conscious of the need for protecting themselves and the information they carried, formed their own symbolism. In much the same way, during the Second World War, many codes were formed to protect the passage of information, similarly various symbols were formed, mainly again an amalgamation of other preceeding ideas, to form new symbols for letters, ideas and thoughts. Most common at that time were the two organisations known as the Inquisition and the Vehmgericht, and their coding systems, although complicated, are well worth taking the trouble to study from the symbolic viewpoint. Codes are still widely used, especially so for the protection of information, and new symbols are, no doubt, being formed all the time.

Sigils

The formation of sigils, mentioned earlier, continues, with many creating their own personal sigils as representative of their magical intentions. Images are created from various symbols, which do not

immediately make the conscious mind connect with the intention, but which do connect at a deeper, subconscious level. There are varying ways of creating sigils, one of which is to write down the intention or desire you have, let's say 'I want to be loved by someone who I in turn love'. If you then take away from that sentence all the letters which are repeated, you end up with a jumble of letters which you can then overlay, one on top of the other, to form a sigil. In this case, we would end up with the letters IWANTOBELVDYSMHUR. Having written this out, decided whether you feel you need to charge it up with power (one of the ways of doing this is to visualise it taking an active form), you could then have it made up into a jewellery form, or just keep the piece of paper with you, and even consider putting it under your pillow at night.

GEOMETRIC SYMBOLS AND SIGNS

*G*eometric symbols and signs form positive shapes, whether *seemingly mathematical or quite abstract. Other than the dot, most geometric symbols can be seen to have grown from three basic types of symbol – the circle, the vertical line and the horizontal line. Thinking back to early civilisations, it is easy to see why these three basic symbols were used. The circle was representative of the Sun, something early humans would see as a small object in the distance, or conversely the Moon. The horizontal line obviously represented the horizon, whilst the vertical line was similar to that of the tree. From these three basic symbols have grown many others, and we are going to take a look at a few of these. This is not an exhaustive list of symbols, but is merely a starting point from which to work for the future.*

DOT

A dot can be of any size, either small or quite large. It is emblematic of the seed, the new beginning, the start of something, the origin, the birth and unity, which is quite the opposite to the thought of a dot as a full stop ending a sentence. The dot as a seed can be actual or imagined, as in the seed of an idea, waiting to bear fruit. It can also be seen as the core of something, a singular thing, which can be the centre of something drawn around it. When, for example, one draws a circle around a dot, it then becomes an astrological symbol for the Sun. It also resembles the eye, with the pupil as its centre, but more of that later.

The dot is also a widely used form within geomancy, an ancient system of prediction, where in some cases, stones, nuts or seeds are thrown on to the earth or on to a special tray and then 'read'. Another form of geomancy is the pricking of marks on paper with a pin, making dots, or even using dice and reading the pattern of dots which result. Dice, which in one form or another, have existed since at least 2000 BCE are in our modern age associated with games, but many still use the system of dots for predictive purposes: dominoes, for instance, can be traced back as far as twelfth-century China, where they were used in prediction. One particular form of geomancy called 'Napoleon's Book of Fate' was used extensively in the nineteenth century, in which various dots are interpreted, although its connection with Napoleon has never been totally proven. There are various theories about this system's origins, but as the oldest surviving text showing this system was written in German and discovered in Napoleon's cabinet of curiosities, it has always been ascribed to Napoleon. Other theories, however, suggest that it was originally part of a hieroglyphic scroll discovered in 1801 by Napoleon's armies.

It is also worthwhile noting that a system of dots is used frequently to show the outline of stars and formations.

HORIZONTAL LINE

Representative in the West of the female and negative principles of matter, this symbol is all about balance and rationale. When you weigh something, you are basically trying to get both sides of the scale to form a straight line, and much is the same with the meaning of the horizontal line. Finding a level, being settled yet being patient for the correct outcome are all associated with the horizontal line, as is the thought of the static, unmoving force. The horizontal line can also form something which joins two vertical lines together, as in the steps of a ladder or in a bridge, when it then takes on the added meaning of attaining something higher than perhaps the limitation to which we are subjected. The horizontal line forms the roof of a building, or the seat of a chair, or even flatness of the Earth's surface itself. Consequently, the horizontal line is very much associated with stability, protection and support. One could, conversely, also see it as a protection from instability.

Those who are familiar with the *I Ching* or *Chinese Book of Changes*, the subject of another book within this series, will be aware that the horizontal line, in both broken and unbroken forms, is the means for drawing hexagrams. To the Chinese, the unbroken, horizontal line, is a masculine force, positive, active and given the polarity of yang, which in turn relates to the Sun, to daytime and to the heavens. On the other hand, the broken line, or yin, is considered to be the passive and feminine, which in turn relates to the Moon, and thus intuitive matters, to the Earth and to the night.

VERTICAL LINE

I

The vertical line, seen as the tree by primitive humans, is consequently something which has 'grown' from the dot, or seed. In most cultures, the vertical line is considered to be masculine, dynamic, positive and active. In its upright position, it is also something which goes both up and down, joining the heavens to the Earth.

We have relied upon trees for fuel, shelter and for the very air we breathe since the dawning of time, and only now are beginning to realise the importance of trees – the growing interest in the Amazon rain forests, for example. Tree worship is something which can be found in nearly every culture, and central to most is the thought of the Tree of Life. Known under this title to those familiar with the Qabalah, by the name Yggdrasil to those familiar with runes or by the name Gnarl to others, the tree not only gives food from the fruits that it can produce, but its leaves shelter us, its bark and roots can be used as medicines, its very fibres can be used for fuel or for shelter, and its branches can be used for making implements as diverse as baskets and arrows. It is no wonder that ancient humans placed so much emphasis on trees, or that the vertical line has always been considered an important symbol. Trees have also been

considered things which unite the Earth and the heavens, and as such sacred groves and forests have developed. When drawing a tree, many people start with the vertical line, so it is not surprising that this line is heavily associated with trees and implements made from them, such as wands, staves, etc. We will be looking at all these, as well as discussing trees in greater detail later.

When children draw the human form, they tend to draw 'stick people'. These people are formed from a vertical straight line, and as such the vertical line, representative perhaps of the spine of the body, is heavily associated with humankind. The spine, which itself helps to protect the internal organs and is the central point of the nervous system, is also thought by many cultures to be the source of the kundalini, the body's energy system.

The vertical line also connects with phallic symbolism (again a masculine principle) and thus with fertilisation, whilst to students of runic symbolism, the rune Isa, shown as a vertical line, means standstill, ice and restriction, something which precedes a rebirth, in much the same way as the ice of winter gives way to the thaw of spring, and the resultant flourishing of flora.

A vertical line forms our letter I and the number 1. It also features widely in many alphabets, especially the Greek. Forming the letter Iota, the ancient Greeks considered it to be representative of destiny or fate, and as such to the goddess of fate, Ananke, and to the three fates. It is also a prominent feature of the Ogham script. The origin of this form of writing is unsure, but it is certain that it was used by Celtic people within the British Isles and ceased to be in use around the seventh century CE. There are many fine examples of Ogham script still available for inspection, including a lovely stone in Lewannick Church in Cornwall. Clearly used as a mnemonic, a means of helping the memory to retain information, each symbol was associated with a tree (not surprisingly) and given certain human qualities. Further information on the Ogham script and the runic script, to which it is closely aligned, can be obtained from reading *Runes for Beginners*, another book in this series.

As stated earlier, the vertical line can be considered to be representative of many things in most cultures, and can take on the connotation of the staff or stave, wand, needle, rod, or even the arrow. Derivatives from these implements are the conductor's baton, the Royal sceptre and the flute or recorder!

In English courts, rods and staves are a common feature, and the most famous modern stave or rod bearer is probably Black Rod, an officer of the British House of Lords who summons the members of the House of Commons to the Lords to hear the monarch's speech from the throne. He raps on the door to gain the attention of those within the chamber with the ebony rod, from which he gets his title.

Linked with power and with protection, the stave has historically not only been used as a weapon, or as a means of defence or support, but also as a marker – it is known that Stone Age people often used staves as marker points. Evidence of the staff or stave's use as a support can be seen in the Bible at the time of Moses. The Bible tells us that Aaron, the first High Priest of the Israelites threw his staff on the ground at the court of the Egyptians, to see it turned into a snake.

Used heavily within Egyptian symbolism, the staff or stave is seen as a connection between heaven and Earth, in much the same way as the vertical line, and it is interesting to note that the gods of many cultures are pictured as holding or having staves, the Japanese, Chinese, Incas, Romans, Greeks, Egyptians being but a few.

Mythology would suggest that Joseph of Arimathea, when he travelled through Europe, met with King Arviragus at a place unknown (thought by some to be the legendary Avalon, which many consider to be Glastonbury), and planted his stave at the summit of a hill. According to legend, the stave then transformed into a thorn tree which blossoms every Christmas Day. In the Qabalah and the study of the Tree of Life, the sceptre is commonly linked with Chesed or Kaph and the spear with Geburah.

Wands, or staves of witches and wizards are quite familiar to us, and most magicians, especially children's entertainers, will be seen to have a 'magic wand', which behaves as a living thing, giving the ability to create – in much the same way as the tree is a living thing, which has the power to grow and create leaves and shelter. Within mystical rituals, the wand, used by the High Priestess, is pointed to

the north, south, east and west, symbolic of the elements of Earth, Air, Fire and Water, and then a circle drawn on the earth for protection. The wand is said to be associated with Fire and with the south, and is a associated in the Qabalah with Yud. Wands have long been symbolic of power and wisdom. To students of the tarot, the wand is actively associated with the suit of the same name in the minor arcana. Wands, also sometimes called sceptres, rods, batons or clubs correspond to clubs in the standard pack of playing cards, and are usually symbolic of hard work and effort – success but not through an easy path. In Buddhism, the wand corresponds to the World Tree, although it is usually illustrated with a serpent entwined around it.

CIRCLE

Symbolic of the Sun in the main part, especially by those who are familiar with the planetary sign for the Sun (a circle with a dot in the middle), this is a symbol of the fifth element Spirit, or of heaven or the heavens, and something which goes way back in time as a symbol, probably to the Paleolithic period. To the Assyrians, the winged circle was representative of the god Asshur, whilst to Zoroastrians, the same kind of winged circle is representative of the god Ashura Mazda. To students of tarot, the Sun symbol itself, being one of the major arcana cards, is representative of the higher self, of the life-force, of safety, happiness and pleasure, and it is interesting to note that the word 'zodiac' actually means circle of animals. All planets are circular in shape, and in nature there are many things which radiate from the circle – flowers, for example, have petals coming from a circular central point, and circles form the central part of the tree-trunk. In many other ways we see the circle in everyday life – clock faces are usually circular, mazes are mainly circular, the wheel is obviously circular, within cathedrals the rose window is circular – the list is virtually endless.

43

The circle is also symbolically representative of nothing (as in zero), of Planet Earth itself, and of a void – a nothing enclosed by a something. It also gives a power to a number it precedes – ten is obviously greater than one. Circles have no start and no finish, much the same as space, of which this is also symbolic. Often, we use the expression 'having come full circle' meaning that we have moved forwards to seemingly come back to the same point. Circles are total, complete, and are also symbolic of movement (as in the wheel, more of which later). Circles are also associated with coins and money, and thus with materialism and earthly things, whereas to students of psychology, the circle represents the self. Considered to be a feminine symbol, the circle is something which appears in many religious and magical ceremonies, and many sacred dances are performed within circles, the dances themselves often being considered to be a sign of a strong community and unbroken tradition. Obviously, the circle is also concerned with movement, possibly because circular things can be made to move unhindered (try rolling something square and see how far it travels).

Considered by Plato to be representative of the psyche, the circle is felt by students of Jungian psychology to represents the self or the totality of the psyche, whilst students of Zen consider it as a symbol of enlightenment, possibly because the Sun and Moon are circular and both shed light on the Earth. Circles are also the same as rings, these standing for eternal, unbroken love, in much the same way as the circle is eternal and has no breaks within it.

Students of the Qabalah will readily appreciate that the circle is connected with Malchuth, whilst students of the tarot will know that coins, also sometimes called circles, pentacles, discs or deniers are another suit, corresponding to the suit of diamonds in the standard playing card pack. Concerned with materialistic matters and financial affairs, this suit also corresponds to the Earth signs of Capricorn, Virgo and Taurus in astrology.

Like the ouroboros, the circle creates itself by eating itself; it has no beginning and no end, it is limitless, and it is worthwhile noting that in folklore, circles drawn around the beds of the ill and of nursing mothers were thought to protect them against demonic attack.

Representative to some as the Wheel of Life itself, this symbol is associated with reincarnation and rebirth, as is the circular pattern of the yearly cycles. Circles then can represent the cycle of life and death, of fate and time, or karma. They are also associated with the Knights of the Round Table, with crop circles, with shields, with protection – in heraldry the circle is known as a roundel or bezant, in a golden form. Early humans often arranged their encampments in circle shapes; it was an enclosure, a protection, facing as it did all directions equally, enclosing the space in which the people lived. It is not surprising that stone circles have featured in human history, when one considers that many cave entrances are round, and in fact we all come from the womb, which to outward appearances, when pregnant, presents a round shape.

If you know about witches, witchcraft and magical rites, the circle is a familiar concept, again symbolic of wholeness and also with the womb of the Earth and the continuing cycle of seasons and birth-death-rebirth. The magic circle is used for the rites at Sabbats and Esbats, and is something which gives protection, as well as something which contains, giving a sacred and purified space. Considered to be an important base, a symbol of eternity, with links to both worlds, it symbolises perfection and wholeness, the actual rituals in creating the circle being very important. Some witches would assert that when working in the circle, they are a part of neither world, but separate to both.

Circles feature in paganism, while the American Indian tradition has its medicine wheels. These are large stone circles, dating possibly as far back as 440 BCE, the most spectacular being the Bighorn Medicine Wheel, which can be found at the summit of Medicine Mountain in Bighorn Mountains of Wyoming. Again considered to be something providing protection, power and spirituality, the medicine wheel is now used mainly for ceremonial purposes.

The circular shape is also the shape of the *mandala*, a Sanskrit word meaning centre, circumference or magic circle. In both Hinduism and Buddhism, the mandala has religious ritualistic purposes, and mandalas feature heavily in the Tibetan Buddhist traditions: it also appears in Christianity and in Gnosticism and many other religions, traditions and mythologies. Carl Jung, who studied not only the I Ching, but also mandalas and varying forms of symbolism in depth, noted that in medieval Christian artwork as well as in the works of alchemy, the mandala featured strongly. In the Christian artwork, it was often shown as Christ at the centre, surrounded by four evangelists at the cardinal points, in much the same way as within Egyptian artwork, Horus was portrayed surround by his four sons also at the cardinal points.

Jung felt that the actual drawing of a mandala was a therapeutic exercise. All that is needed to form a mandala are a circle with a central focal point: the circle is eternity, and the central point symbolises unity, an element of independence, perfection, beginning and in many cases, God. Mandalas have many uses in meditation and in visualisation techniques, and often appear with other forms inside or outside of them – sometimes a square is drawn around the outside of the circle, or there may be squares inside the circle. Triangles also feature in mandalas, and the directional element is quite important. We will be discussing the use of mandalas in meditation in a later chapter.

Other forms of symbol

We have covered the basic symbols, but from these many others have evolved. We will now take a look at some these. Again, this is not an exhaustive list or set of descriptions. It leaves room for further study to evolve.

The caduceus

Known not only to the Egyptians, but also to the Greeks and Indians who used the symbol at the entrance to temples, the caduceus is a combination of the vertical line with two spirals and a winged disc. Said to originate in Mesopotamia, where it was considered to be a symbol of the god who cured illness, it is seen by some to be a stick upon which a serpent is climbing, and as such to be representative of

the kundalini, or energy force, rising up the spine to energise each chakra centre it encounters en route. The serpent, about which we have already learnt, also connects with regeneration, and thus with health, and it is not surprising that the Greek god of healing, Ascelpius, is closely connected with snakes and the caduceus, and that it is still used today as the symbol for physicians. Asclepius, was, incidentally, also connected with dogs and it is interesting to note that Quetzalcoatl, the Aztec serpent god whose priests were also physicians, had a mythical twin called Xolotl, who was also a dog!

Traditionally, the spiralling serpents represent male and female, unconscious and conscious, and thus are complementary. In addition, associated as it is with healing, it is also symbolic of the Hippocratic Oath, Hippocrates incidentally being a great believer in the power of astrology.

To the Egyptians, the caduceus represented Thoth, the Egyptian equivalent of Mercury (messenger to the gods, and thus connected with communication) and Hermes, who it was believed formed the Earth with his spoken word. Thoth was not only scribe to the gods, but also lord of medicine, and thus learning, healing, literary ability and justice, as well as magic to some degree, are all associated with the caduceus. With regard to Mercury, legend suggests that he tried to stop two serpents fighting, and they wound themselves round his staff instead, thus forming the caduceus. To the Romans, the caduceus symbolised good conduct and moral righteousness, and it is still used as an insignia by the Catholic bishop in the Ukraine. The vertical line symbolic in this instance of spirit or of the god descends into matter, shown by the crossing of the four spirals which in turn represent the four elements. The spirals also represent the yin and yang, passive and active, and thus duality, and this leads the caduceus to be a powerful image to use in meditation, especially when there is a need to obtain balance, or problems with communication exist (the Mercury connection).

The winged disc at the top of the caduceus is thought to be symbolic of the crown chakra or of the enlightenment which we all strive to attain. To students of the Qabalah, the caduceus is linked with Beth. Generally, the caduceus is said to symbolise strength, knowledge, understanding, commercial success, self-control, and good health, the latter possibly due to its links with medicine and healing.

CROSS

One form of cross is that shown above – a symbol of Christianity; we really need to take a detailed look at the cross and at crucifixion to fully understand its significance, the various types of cross, and their meanings. It is a well-established fact that the cross, symbolic of the death of Jesus, was used as a symbol many thousands of years before the setting up of the Christian Church, and many Bible students feel that the symbol of the cross, being pagan in origin, should not be associated with Jesus Christ or true forms of Christianity.

The crucifix which many wear as a symbol of their belief is carried by more people than any other religious talisman, and is considered by many to be sacred: people sometimes go far as to make the cross an object of adoration or an icon in its own right. Indeed since the time of Jesus' death, the object on which he died has been depicted

in many ways. People seeking to trace the actual form of the cross or torture stake have looked back at the original Greek scriptures where the word *stauros* is used, and concluded that this means any upright wooden stake firmly fixed in the ground. This could mean any implement at all, such as a pole in a fence, but further investigations have revealed that the word 'stauros' also indicates something used for impalement of human beings. In many cases, especially during the time of the Roman Empire, the execution stake became a vertical pole with a horizontal crossbar placed at some point, and although the period of time at which this happened is uncertain, what is known is that simple impalement became known as crucifixion.

Tau

T

One of the oldest types of cross symbol is the Tau, or St Anthony's cross, which is shaped like a letter T. Forming part of many alphabets, the Tau was considered by the early Greeks to be linked with the Moon, and also to have links with man (a man standing legs together, with arms outstretched). To early Christians, however, it was seen to link to the Trinity (having three directions). Generally, it is considered to be representative of purity of thought and authority, and is associated with anything religious or relating to the well-being of humankind as a whole. Formerly considered to be a powerful protection against diseases such as epilepsy, and thus a symbol of healing, medicine and nursing, and also used as a preventive against the effects of a snake bite, this symbol is often associated, because of its Christian linkage, with eternal life, and has over the centuries often been used as a protection against trouble and strife. The Tau is considered by Qabalists particularly to be representative of the Tree of Life and Lamed, and by the Mayas as regeneration and hidden wisdom. Those familiar with runic symbolism will associate this type of cross with the hammer of Thor, the god of thunder.

Upward pointing arrow

In fact, in many cases, with just a slight alteration in form, this cross can easily be the runic symbol Tir, shown by the arrow pointing upwards, symbolic of the warrior, victory in battle and the guiding star. Symbolically, this sort of heavenly pointing arrow is thought to represent the ascent of a soul to the heavens, as well as obviously indicating a direction. Arrows, however, can have a phallic significance and also a romantic significance, as in the drawings lovers often do of a heart pierced by an arrow, actually symbolising the piercing by a masculine object of a feminine principle. We will discuss hearts as symbols later on.

Y-shaped cross

The y-shaped cross is similar to the runic symbol for Algiz – one vertical line through which a V shape is inserted at the top. Again thought of as similar to the shape of the Tree of Life, this type of cross is felt to symbolise a ladder by which we may reach God. However, to students of the runes, this symbol means protection, and to students of ancient Greek, it represents Ypsilon, which stands for water, itself often a protection against invaders. It is interesting to realise that when this symbol is reversed and encircled, it becomes the symbol internationally associated with CND.

Latin cross

In the latin cross, a horizontal crossbar intersects the upright beam somewhere along its upper half. This symbol is often used as the Christian crucifix, following the theories put forward by theologian Irenaeus (120–202 CE). Archelolgy gives us a clue about the kinds of

crosses used during the time of Jesus by the Roman authorities. In June 1968, a tomb or depository for the bones of the dead was discovered north of Jerusalem in an area known as Ammunition Hill. Containing the bones of a young man who had obviously been crucified, possibly between 7 CE and 66 CE, the remains included the victim's two heel bones fastened together by a nail. His arms, not his hands, were nailed to the crossbar. The weight of the man's body was borne by a plank nailed to the upright beam which would have supported his bottom, his legs were bent at the knees and both legs were broken, as were the legs of the two criminals put to death at the same time as Jesus (John 19:32). As a result of this discovery, theologians now conclude that if Jesus died in a similar fashion, then his legs were not fully extended as is portrayed in most artwork. It is also felt that the man's feet were probably only inches away from the ground, and if that is so, we must also, then, revise our mental images of the death of Jesus on this point as well.

It is interesting to realise that the crucifixion cross, used originally to punish criminals and thus being connected with wrongdoing now signifies the ultimate martyrdom of one's self, the sacrificing of one's life. It is also worthwhile noting that many churches use the cross shape as a plan for their building.

The cross, being symbolic to many as an emblem of Christianity and the love of Christ, when dissected merely becomes two lines. The vertical line, when considered as a pole or stake, is felt to be representative of our desire and need to delve deeper within ourselves, in much the same way as the stake is driven deep within the earth. The crossbar, being fairly high up on the vertical stake is felt to be representative of higher forms and higher teachings, and as such its religious use is quite appropriate.

SWORD

The shape of the Latin cross is also similar in design to that of the sword, which is an important symbol itself, and emblematic of fighting, warfare and the pursuit of freedom, as well as death and destruction. Indeed many societies, both present and past, venerate the sword as a symbol, and oriental bishops wear the sword as part of their ceremonial dress as a religious symbol of liberty and strength through God, of war and of peace. Qabalists will automatically link the sword with Pe. Swords incidentally form parts of other religious symbolism – the Khanda, for example, being a

symbol of Sikhism. This composes a two-edged sword, a symbol of God's concern for truth and justice, with two other swords which stand for God's power, and a circle, being a sign of the Unity of God, and of eternity. To students of the tarot, however, the sword or epee

is one of the suits of the minor arcarna, and is connected with progress, either for better or worse, opposition, authority and strength through problem solving.

The sword forms a very important part of the rituals of witchcraft, where it is linked with masculinity, a penetrating, separating force, and an obvious phallic connection. Whilst it can be seen that the sword is a weapon which can kill, to pagans this connects to thoughts of life, with animals having always been killed in order to provide life for people, and it is worthwhile remembering that swords, knives and the like can be used equally effectively by women as men. In various rituals, the sword is used by those practising witchcraft.

St Benedict cross

One of the most popular forms of cross in ancient times was the St Benedict cross, which was engraved with symbolic letters upon a medallion. It is also fairly common to see this type of cross made from parchment or cardboard, with the cross and initial letters formed from either paint or ink. Thought to protect the wearer from any sort of danger, the letters used in this form of cross are representative of Latin words, which are read as shown below.

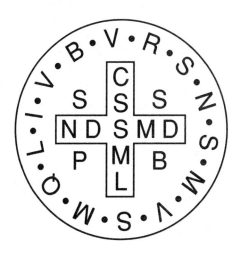

The four letters in the angles of the cross:
Crux Sancti Patris Benedicti (Cross of the Holy Father Benedict)

The four letters in the upright bar:
Crux Sancta sit mihi lux (O Holy Cross be my light)

The four letters in the horizontal:
Ne daemon sit mihi dux (Let no evil spirit be my guide)

The circle of letters: *Vade retro Satana*
                        (Get thee behind me Satan)
                        Ne suade mihi vana
                        (Suggest no vain delusions to me)
                        Sunt mala quae libas
                        (The things you offer are evil)
                        Ipse venana bibas
                        (You yourself drink poison)

The St Benedict cross is usually depicted in the form of what is known as the Greek cross, similar to the + sign, used in mathematics as a form of addition, and also known as the equal-armed cross. The joining of the vertical and horizontal lines is said to represent the joining of spiritual things with material, and this form of cross is the universal symbol of man, indicative of man's abilities and desires to push himself in all possible directions, and symbolic of change. With the lines intersecting from different directions, this sign is considered to be a union of opposites, showing the four cardinal points, four elements, four dimensions and anything related to the number four. Within paganism, the number four is also a very important factor, there being four major festivals or Sabbats, which mark the seasons.

When encircled, the Greek cross is also known as the Celtic cross, the Lodge cross or the Solar Wheel, thought to symbolise the containing of religious force, power, law and order. It symbolises the Earth as a material and physical existence, and in general the encircling of the cross shape stands for the eternal preservation of life. Taking the circle, however, and putting it at the centre of the cross, you find the symbol of the chakra a prominent part of Hindu teachings, and well known to those who are students of the esoteric or of healing. Representative of the unity of the four elements, this

combination of cross with wheel shows divinity combined with sacrifice, but also conveys the sense of movement forwards. Similarly, the Wheel of the Law which contains two intersecting crosses within a circle, is a symbol of Buddhism, the rim of the wheel standing for the cycle of birth, death and reincarnation, and each spoke symbolic of an action which a Buddhist should practise to escape from the eternal cycle. The centre point symbolises peace, at which time the soul reaches Nirvana, and is not subject to another earthly existence. We will be discussing wheels in greater detail later.

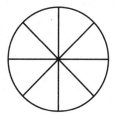

St Andrew's cross

Depicted thus ✕ the St Andrew's cross is another popular type of cross, and is also known as the crux decussata, or as the saltire cross or Patrick's cross (notice that both St Andrew of Scotland and St Patrick of Ireland both 'claim' this symbol). Symbolic of the union of the Upper World with the Lower World, or of the spiritual with the material, this type of cross has long been regarded as a protection against evil, and has associations with the number 10, which is considered the number of totality, completion of cycles, regeneration and regrowth. To students of the runes, this type of cross mean partnership or gift, and is given the name Gebo. To lovers, however, it is a sign of the kiss, and similarly to the ancient Greeks for whom it formed the letter Chi it signified the cosmos, or to individuals, private property, as well as being the symbol of the gift. Two such crosses placed one above the other form the runic sign of Ing, symbolic of fertility and new beginnings, seen by many to be linked with the new Moon and with intuition.

Split-armed cross

The split-armed cross is slightly different from the equal-armed cross in that each arm is split at its end, giving a cross with eight points. Used at the times of the crusades, it is interesting to realise that those of Islamic faith readily accept that there are eight divisions of space and eight angels holding up the world. The crusaders may have developed this type of cross to symbolise their own cause, having met with the thoughts of Islam.

Multi-armed cross

The multi-armed cross with its six directions, can also be easily turned into a star shape (see below) and is well known to most people as the shape of the weather vane, itself considered to be representative of the universe.

Eight-armed cross

The eight-armed cross or double cross is considered to be connected to the Sun, whilst to students of runic symbolism it is connected with the eight legs of Odin's horse, Sleipnir, and the eight corners of heaven.

OTHER TYPES OF CROSS

Type of cross

Meaning

Arrow-headed cross
or cross barby

Centrifugal forces.
Cross barby in Christendom
symbolises fish spears and
links with the disciples
as fishers of men.

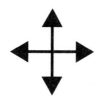

Double cross
or passion cross

Parallel forces.
Passion cross in Christendom
symbolises Christ's suffering,
and is thus also known as
the Cross of Suffering.

Maltese cross

Eight directions, forces
emanating from the centre.

Cross of the Knights Templar

Parts of a circle (note the
rounded edges) working from
a central force.

Teutonic cross

Composed of triangles (see below) this symbolises higher ideals.

Lunate cross

Representative of the phases of the Moon, and seen by some as forming a pagan link.

Rose cross or cross of ovals

Symbolic of secrets and silence, the four petals represent the cosmos. To Qabalists, this cross links with Tiph-Ereth.

OTHER CROSSES OF CHRISTENDOM

Type of cross	Meaning
Cross cordee	Symbolic of the ropes with which Christ was bound.

Chain Cross

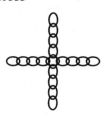

Symbolic of the chains of sin which can be broken only by the cross.

Cross engrailed

Symbolic of the sharpness and thorniness of pain.

Cross pattee

Symbolic of the sheltering wings representative of the protective power of the cross.

Moving on from the cross, we come across two interconnected symbols.

SWASTIKA OR FYLFOT

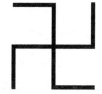 

This symbol is probably one of the oldest, and is found, not only in Nazi history, but in most of the ancient cultures, from the orient through Hinduism and Islam into Scandinavia and Europe, and in fact is linked with Kether in the Qabalistic tradition. The word Swastika, coming from a Sanskrit word meaning 'bringer of good fortune' has long been used to symbolise happiness, good fortune, human progress and longevity. Found in certain Christian catacombs, as well as in pre-Columbian America, this symbol is also sometimes known as the gammadion, because it can be formed by joining up four gamma letters. Associated by many with movement and motion since the Middle Ages, and also connected with the power of the Sun, it is sometimes drawn within a circle, again conveying a sense of movement. Said to be representative of the power of the four winds, it can be drawn in the form of three, five or six human legs. It is said that during the Iron Age the swastika symbol represented God, and it is said to have two forms, the masculine which revolves clockwise and the feminine which revolves anticlockwise. These relate to the solar and lunar aspects. The solar aspect, linking the power of the Sun to regenerate, is a masculine force, thought by many Scandinavians to represent magical powers, control and force. The lunar aspect, feminine and softer in approach, is seen as Nature and growth through Nature.

The Ankh

Possibly one of the most widely recognised symbols other than the cross, sacred to the ancient Egyptians, and often used as an amulet, this symbol is basically the T or Tau cross supporting a circular shape. Giving the appearance of the shape of a key, in Egyptian hieroglyphics this symbol stands for life or living, and forms part of

the Egyptian words such as 'health' and 'happiness'. Linked with Egyptian gods and goddesses, such as Isis (eternal mother and High Priestess) and Osiris, most gods would appear to have possessed the ankh, to symbolise life and immortality, and it is thus often referred to as the Key of Life, or even the cross of life, because of its creative power. The loop of the ankh is considered to be the feminine, whilst the T shape is considered to be the masculine. Together, these symbols reflect a continued existence.

Many illustrations of Egyptian gods show them wearing or carrying ankhs as an amulet to signify their immortality. Combining the eternal with the physical, this symbol being both male and female, is worn by both sexes as an amulet. If you are unfamiliar with the word amulet, it is basically a protector, or something which is considered to bring good luck to the wearer. Coming from the Latin word *amuletum*, meaning 'means of defence', amulets are always considered to have inherent protective qualities, and have been used by many civilisations, not only the Egyptians who would have always had at least one amulet each, usually in the form of ornate jewellery, in their households. Kings were given an amulet of an ankh by birthright. A talisman, however, is a specific charm meant to have a specific purpose – such as attracting monetary gain, or helping to attract a partner. It is well known that many witches wear the ankh as a protector. An amulet of an ankh was given to all those who died, who, after their Day of Judgment, were found righteous.

To some, the ankh signifies the Sun rising over the horizon, and thus regeneration, regrowth and renewal, whilst to others it resembles the human being, with arms extended, the loop representative of the head. It is, interestingly, also the plan used by many churches and cathedrals rather than the standard crucifix.

Considered by many to have powerful protective qualities, this symbol is actively associated with health, prosperity and long life at every level.

STAR

To many, stars are synonymous with hope and with idealism. This probably stems from the Biblical account of the 'three wise men' who followed the star, hopeful that it would lead them to the baby Jesus. To students of the tarot, however, the star is one of the cards forming part of the major arcarna, pointing the way to an easier existence, given that we have faith and hope.

Early civilisations had star-gods, the Babylonians being just one. Stars are depicted with any number of points. However, most stars are normally five, six, seven, nine or twelve-pointed. You may be aware that stars with an uneven number of points can be drawn with one continuous line, whilst those with an even number of points consist of a series of interlinked triangles (see below). To most people, the star is a symbol of light, spirituality, the heavens and peace.

fIVE-POINTED STAR

The most common type of star is the five-pointed star, with two of the points forming the base. Sometimes called the pentagram, especially in witchcraft when a circle is also drawn around it (a pentacle), it is occasionally shown with rays emerging from it, and thus given the name of The Flaming Star, symbolic of the mystic. The five-pointed star can actually be traced as far back as the days of the Pharoahs, when it symbolised the rising up of the spirit to the heavens, and the power of the Earth; to the Greeks it was a symbol of Demeter's daughter Kore, the goddess of vegetation, possibly because the apple contains a star composed of five seeds in its core. To Qabalists, the five-pointed star is linked with Geburah, and is symbolic of the five senses, and of human limbs, whilst to students of Pythagorus, it was called the Pentalpha, because it was seen to be composed of five interwoven alpha letterings – alpha standing represents new starts, beginnings and birth, with the centre linked to the sixth sense and the unconscious. When two such five-pointed stars are linked, they are connected to Malchuth, and are symbolic of the five human limbs in an upright position (head, two arms and two legs).

Commonly associated with creation and spirituality, the five-pointed star is frequently used as a symbol of protection and healing, considered to carry immense power for good, and protecting not only physical well-being, but also mental and spiritual. Drawn with

one continuous stroke, the most common way of showing the five-pointed star is with a single point uppermost. When inverted, the five-pointed star is often associated with black magic, spells and the elements, and students of numerology will know that the number five is also the number of magic. Linked in witchcraft to the four elements of Air, Earth, Fire and Water plus the fifth element of Ether of Spirit, when shown with the single point upwards, it represents the power of the mind working with the material.

The five-pointed star is very popular in pagan jewellery and especially popular with witches, who liken it to the disk which appears on Wiccan altars as symbolic of the Earth. Followers of what is known as 'the craft' or the 'old tradition' will use the symbol of the pentacle as often as possible, feeling that it helps to draw to them the energy and wisdom needed to operate effectively in the modern world.

Six-pointed star

The six-pointed Star of David, or hexagram, symbolising Judaism is familiar to most of us. The menorah or seven-branched candlestick is also heavily featured in the study of the Qabalah. This star shape is actually made up of two opposed interlaced triangles, and Jews have actually been using this symbol for only a relatively short time, although is appears to have no actual religious meaning. This symbol has been in existence for many thousands of years, and is thought to be useful as a protector. To those who study paganism or witchcraft, it symbolises the spreadeagled male body, and being made of two equilateral interlaced triangles, it also shows a balance between masculinity and femininity, the upward pointing triangle being symbolic of man and the downward pointing triangle being symbolic of woman. For the Jews, this star has an emotional impact. During the Second World War, Jews in countries controlled by the Nazis were forced to wear this sign on their clothing as a method of identification. To many, especially those of Polish origin, this gave them the opportunity to turn a negative situation into something more positive – they used costly materials to make their Star of David, thus making it a symbol of pride in being Jewish. Thought to be representative of Fire and Water, active and passive, positive and negative, heaven and Earth, this symbol became connected with thoughts of peace, perfect balance and the union of the higher and lower selves which everybody strives to attain. To students of yoga, this shape represents the heart centre in the chakras, and the powers of the air. The number 6, linking with Venus and with love, is also considered to be the number of balance and harmony, and linking with the colour indigo, is considered to be a very spiritual number. This double triangle is connected to the desire to share and the desire to receive, and Qabalists will link it to Tiph-Ereth.

SEVEN-POINTED STAR

The seven-pointed star is also known as the Seal of Solomon, and is actively associated with those who seek out wisdom and the truth. The Seal of Solomon is thought by Qabalists to have developed from the Star of David, with a point of spirit in the centre (6 + 1), and it is thought by many to be symbolic of the absolute, the all powerful, and to protect those who carry it against all harm. Many theories have been expounded about the meaning behind seven-pointed stars, and it is thought by some, following a theory put forward by Professor Thom, to be the geometric basis of the stone circle at Moel

Ty Uchaf in North Wales. Students of numerology will well be aware that according to Cheiro, it contains the number 9, symbolic of humankind, and also links with the planets. Starting clockwise, these points begin Sun, Mars, Jupiter, Saturn, Moon, Mercury, Venus and back to the Sun. The lines go Sun, Moon, Mars, Mercury, Jupiter, Venus and Saturn – said to be the cycle of life.

Nine-pointed star

The nine-pointed star is well known in astronomy as relating to the sixty-year major aspect cycle between Saturn and Jupiter, which started in Capricorn in 1901 and moved through the zodiac back to Capricorn in 1961. To Qabalists, anything relating to the number 9 is associated with God, but to students of numerology, it is representative of humankind.

Twelve-pointed star

The twelve-pointed star also has astrological connections, being related to the twelve signs of the zodiac. It also connects with the twelve disciples, the twelve knights of the Round Table, the twelve tribes of Israel and the twelve months of the year. This star, made up of four interlaced triangles, links the four elements of Fire, Earth, Air and Water.

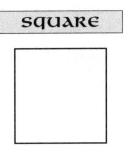

SQUARE

Made up of four straight lines of equal lengths, this is symbolic of totality and order, as well as limitations, hence the thought that the square, forming a box, can be a container as well as something which prevents escape (hence the saying 'I feel boxed in').

Connected with the material rather than the spiritual, this is a symbol of solidity – houses are basically square shapes – firmness, stability and security, whilst to some, the square will represent the Earth, not as a planet but as a materialistic existence. This is especially so in India, where anything cube-shaped is symbolic of Earth, and is given a feminine connection.

Most children will draw cars as box shapes with circles for wheels; again a material connection. The square is connected with the number 4, and students of numerology will already understand the feeling of security and practicality associated with the number, and link this with the four seasons, and four quarters of the Moon, whilst those familiar with the works of psychologist Carl Jung will possibly consider the square to symbolise the inner state of man, who has not, as yet, found himself.

To the Egyptians, the square was symbolic of achievement. If you turn the square round through 45 degrees, it becomes a diamond shape, representative of the feminine principle, also known as the yoni. Connected with money and again with materialism ('diamonds are a girl's best friend'), it also connects with playing cards (diamond suit).

In its three-dimensional form, the four lines of the square also make up the cube, which is connected with the number 8 and with eternity, as well as with the kundalini. Interestingly, the number 8, itself a symbol, indicates two spheres, the material and the spiritual, and is connected with Hod in the Qabalistic tradition.

TRIANGLE

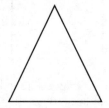

This common form of joining together three lines is well known in mathematical circles. and is most commonly seen with all sides

having an equal length (equilateral triangle). Like the circle, it is also actively used in everyday symbolism, for example in washing instructions as well as in road signs. Triangles are, obviously, associated with the number 3 and everything to which this relates, from the Trinity through to higher consciousness, whilst to put a circle around a triangle symbolises containment within the circle of eternity. To students of psychology, placing a triangle, apex uppermost, between a circle and a square, represents communication, whilst to alchemists, a triangle without its apex was a symbol of air. However, a triangle with its apex uppermost is representative of the Sun, of the male principle and of the element of Fire. It is often used within meditation as an aid to focus, and is purported to be representative of the higher self and of the spirit as a whole. When bisected by a horizontal line, the upward pointing triangle symbolises the element of Air, whilst if inverted, a similar triangle represents the element of Earth. A downward pointing triangle signifies the element of Water, female in principle and lunar in aspect. It is seen as receptive, the source of wisdom and is often used in meditation when answers to questions are required.

The number 3, sometimes symbolic of man, wife and child, is also obviously symbolic of anything relating to the Trinity and within paganism to the Triple Goddess (Maiden, Mother and Crone).

Used within the Greek alphabet as representing Delta, the ancient Greeks considered it to be symbolic of all four elements – Earth, Air, Fire and Water, and thus with the number 4 and all its links, as well as with completion and wholeness.

The right-angled triangle (Pythagorean) was a very important symbol to the ancient Egyptians, who regarded the vertical as representative of the male, the horizontal as the female, and the hypotenuse as the offspring of the two. This triangle is the basis of the Golden Mean on which all balanced architecture was based.

Triangles are sometimes used in paganism for evocation.

Three triangles interlaced together are symbolic of the Trinity, the number 9 (3 × 3) and also with creativity – pregnancy tests for nine months, whilst to students of the runes, this is symbolic of Valknutr, the knot of the fallen or chosen ones, showing the cycle of birth-death-new beginnings.

PYRAMID

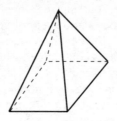

Formed from a combination of the triangle and the square, this symbol is heavily associated with the Egyptians, for obvious reasons, but is also associated with the Qabalah and with Shin. It is also, again, associated with the number 7 because of its links with the triangle (3) and the square (4), but also with the number 5, as it has four corners and an apex. Interestingly, the number 4 connects within the Qabalah with Chesed which is represented in symbolism by both the pyramid and the square, and concerns personal love. As the base of a pyramid is a square shape, this represents earthly things, material concerns and stability. Known also as The Sacred Mountain, the pyramid shape with its steps leading ever upwards to the highest point is representative of the states of consciousness, and is considered to be a place of initiation and a route to attaining a true meditative state. Its triangle shape is considered to correspond with Fire, especially in India and the Far East.

Pyramids have long been held to have special qualities. For example, razor blades placed within the Great Pyramid at Geza remain sharp over decades for reasons as yet unknown to science. Another remarkable power connected with pyramids is the rapid drying out and subsequent mummification of anything organic left within it. Many currently feel that sitting within a pyramid shape will have a beneficial effect on one's mental health, and there are also those who keep a pyramid-shaped object underneath their beds, feeling that it will bring luck and money.

COMBINATION SYMBOLS, ASTROLOGY AND THE PLANETS

In chapter 3, we looked at signs formed from shapes, both mathematical and geometric. In this chapter, we will look at how some of these basic symbols have altered, and how they have grown from a common source. We will also consider the symbolism used within the Western and Chinese astrology systems.

SPIRAL

The spiral is probably one of the most ancient universal symbols known to humankind. Being formed from a single dot, it can be envisaged as having grown from the initial seed, and moved forwards, and as such it is considered to be a symbol of motion, of energy, of evolution. It is also connected with the orbit of the Moon, and with anything which rotates, or rolls up, like scrolls, for example. Associated with the chakras, the spiral also connects with the kundalini and the coiled serpent or snake. Because of the spiral's shape, it is also connected with the labyrinth and with searching. It is shown on weather maps often symbolising a hurricane or whirlwind, and sometimes on a washing machine to show the spin cycle. Similarly because its shape resembles that of a shell and the human ear, it also links with listening and with silence. Many natural forms, both on Earth and out in the galaxies have spiral shapes, and certain traditional dances seem to spiral round, especially those primitive dances associated with healing and magic.

Spirals appear in three forms – the expanding spiral, when it is symbolic of the Sun, the contracting spiral and the ossified spiral, both of which are linked to lunar symbolism.

It is said that when the spiral circles to the right, it is the creative spiral, representative of yang or positive energy, whereas when it circles to the left, it is called the destructive spiral, which represents yin or negative energy.

To the ancient Egyptians, the scroll was symbolic of life, breath and spirit, and the Egyptian god Thoth is often illustrated with a large spiral on his head, symbolic of the snake shape, and not only of his godship, but also of his power.

wheel

Evolving from the circle, the wheel can be depicted either with spokes or without. We have already discussed the wheel briefly in relation to the circle, and discovered that the Wheel of the Law is an essential symbol of Buddhism, whilst the wheel also features in Taoist philosophies. However, the wheel also connects with the Wheel of Life and the Wheel of Fortune, the latter being known to students of the tarot as one of the twenty-two major arcarna cards. The Wheel of Fortune card is connected with progress, changes and new things, and obviously has a connection with gambling and roulette, and so leads on to concerns of a material nature.

The symbolism behind wheels can be quite complex, and there are various thoughts on the meaning behind their use. Those people who think of the wheel as a disk feel it is static, whilst those who think in terms of the wheel itself attribute movement to it. As with the circle, the wheel is representative of the Sun and is connected with light and fire, symbolised in the wheel of fire at some festivals and the Catherine wheel firework.

Wheels generally speaking concern matters of change, of birth and rebirth, or movement, time, fate and karma. It is also thought of as being symbolic of the centre and relating to the cycle of change, the seasons and evolution. The wheel can be directed or move freely, and so symbolically the wheel can relate to freedom from restriction or to moving in a certain, planned, direction. In alchemy, the wheel is symbolic of movement, and of progress or regression. Obviously, wheels can move forwards and backwards. As we have already learnt, the word 'zodiac' refers to a circle, or wheel, of animals, and the Sanskrit word *chakra* also means 'wheel'. As students of yoga or of healing will know, the chakras are the seven energy centres within the body, located along the spine and reaching up to the crown of the head. Further information on chakras can be found in *Spiritual Healing – a beginner's guide*, another book in this series.

LINKED CIRCLES

8 ∞

Two circles joined together are symbolic of the joining together of the masculine with the feminine. They form the figure 8, so they also link with anything with an 8 connotation. When you draw the number 8, you can see that it has no start and no finish, in much the same way as the circle, and as such it is a sign of infinity, especially when drawn sideways on, when it is called the lemniscate. The number 8 also connects with things of a material nature, and with justice. Students of the tarot cards will know that this figure is depicted on the Magician card in many decks, and as such symbolises knowledge, the number 888 in particular was considered by the Greeks to be representative of the higher intelligence (the Greek spelling of Jesus, *Iesous*, works out at 888).

The space where two circles interlace is commonly known as the vesica piscis or vesica mandorla, and symbolically this relates to change on the one part and lack of change on the other. The central, interlaced area, signifies the balance between these two polarities, mediation and resolution. This shape is often found in religious artwork, and is associated with purity. Linking as it does with the elipse, linked circles are also connected with the yoni or diamond shape we have previously mentioned, with fertility and growth and with material concerns.

Linking three circles, one arrives at a symbol of the Trinity, as one would expect with anything associated with the number 3. It also connects with the Round of Enlightenment in Buddhism.

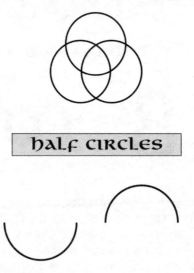

balf circles

Half circles relate to the horseshoe, to rainbows, to the crescent Moon and to the mind and soul. In lunar symbolism, when facing to the left, it is symbolic of the Moon's first quarter, and thus of expansion and growth, strength and power, and considered to offer an element of protection, personal and material advancement. When facing the right, however, it signifies retreat. If facing upwards from the horizontal, it is symbolic of protection and containment, whilst when facing downwards from the horizontal, the shape is connected with water, with nourishment and with receptive ideas. It is also connected, when facing downwards, with the Moon's north node, with prestige and repute, and good fortune. When this half circle is shown in the form of a rainbow, the symbolism revolves around the bridge between heaven and Earth, and concerns both Fire and Water.

RAINBOW

The rainbow shape, itself a semicircle or half circle is said by many to relate to the restoration of order, it being a sign that the rain is to stop and the dry weather return. Similarly, the rainbow can be thought of acting as a bridge between the Earth and the heavens. To those in China, it is also symbolic of the bridge between God and man, a union between heaven and Earth. Likewise the ancient Israelites looked upon the rainbow as a sign of the covenant between God and Noah and his family that, after the flood, 'no more would all flesh be cut off by waters of a deluge, and no more would there occur a deluge to bring the earth to ruin'. Bridges, however, generally speaking are seen as relating to change from one thing to another.

horseshoe

The horseshoe has been used as a symbol of good luck since early Greek times, and is often nailed to the outside of doors, with the end always pointing upwards to contain the good luck. It is said to be truly lucky, one should find the horseshoe personally, rather than buying or acquiring it from other sources. Horseshoes as symbols probably stem from the Egyptian goddess Isis, who had as her symbol the crescent Moon, which was seen to have 'horns'. Roman invaders subsequently 'stole' the symbol, and many Roman women wore crescent Moon shapes on their shoes, feeling that they would be protected from the evil influences thought to be exerted by the Moon itself, and also that it would ensure a happy pregnancy. The crescent Moon is said to be represented by the element of Air, whilst the horseshoe normally corresponds to the element of Earth.

Eventually, the horseshoe itself became used as a similar symbol of good fortune, with the horse considered by many to have magical properties. It is said that Nelson nailed a horseshoe to the mast of his famous ship, *HMS Victory*, and in certain parts of England, the horseshoe is still regarded as being able to protect ships against storms.

ÐIVIÐEÐ CIRCLE

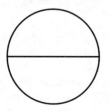

The divided circle is a symbol comprising both the circle and a line cutting across it. If there is a horizontal line across the middle, this indicates division, anything relating to two: two hemispheres, two polarities, etc. It also represents the division between heaven and Earth and between the conscious and unconscious mind. To many, the circle thus divided also shows the connection between the upper and lower worlds, between heaven and hell and consequently between good and evil. Should the circle be divided by a wavy line, or even an S shape, the circle becomes similar to the yin/yang symbol, suggesting forces in perfect balance, as already discussed.

PARALLEL LINES

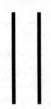

When two parallel lines are depicted, they are symbolic of duality, as one would expect. Parallel lines never come together, running side by side, and remaining totally separate one from the other. As such, they are symbolic of opposites and contrary polarities, but also of balance and equality. In numerology, as well as in mathematics, two parallel lines form the number 11. This can be added together to form the number 2, but in the Pythagorean system, they remain as 11, and as such are considered to be a master number, one showing strength to work through difficulties, hard work and effort. Through its links with columns and pillars, especially of Hermes, Hercules and others, this symbol also links with the zodiac sign for Gemini, the twins, and as such relates again to duality, to communication and the element of fun, as well as to linking opposites and inversion.

PILLARS OR COLUMNS

As we have seen, parallel lines can also be symbolic of pillars, or columns, supporting another structure above and, as such, can often be considered to represent a gateway or entrance to another sphere of existence, being symbolic of eternal stability themselves with the space between being symbolic of the entrance to eternity. Connections with ancient temples are obvious, and many variations of the pillar or column are depicted in ancient artwork. Sometimes, these pillars or columns are coloured, one white and one black, to symbolise good and evil intent; likewise the two columns themselves can be seen to symbolise male and female, negative and positive, life and death, creation and destruction. It is interesting to note from an Egyptian point of view, that the pillar of Osiris was considered to be a symbol of strength and stability. As both a god of fertility and of the underworld, Osiris signified the triumph of life over death. The symbol of Osiris' pillar became regarded as very powerful, the single column being considered as the backbone of the god, in much the same way as we have already seen with the tree. Another Egyptian god to connect with the pillar shape was Anubis, whose symbol of a column, or sometimes also a coffin upon which lay a jackal or Egyptian hunting dog, was thought to protect. Anubis himself, was able to find lost things, as he was an explorer and guide. and thus it is no surprise that he became the patron of psychiatrists!

TRIPLE LINES

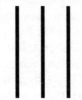

These obviously refer to the Trinity and anything relating to the number 3, from father, mother, child through to body, soul and spirit. If depicted vertically, these also relate to the trident, trefoil and other three-unit forms. The trident and the fleur-de-lis which evolved from it, are symbolic of power and status, both of good and evil intent. The trident, especially, is considered to be representative of Neptune and the devil, who is often depicted in artwork as holding such an implement. The trident is also linked with Shiva the Destroyer. These parallel lines form the number 111, which is considered a number of magic, and used within magic squares – lines of numbers which add the same horizontally, vertically and diagonally. Three triangles are also symbolic of the Trinity, whilst to students of the runic text, three lines signify the knot of the fallen or chosen ones, and are symbolic of evolution, life-death-rebirth. We will be discussing knots in a later chapter.

ASTROLOGICAL SYMBOLISM

We have already made mention of astrological symbols – the Gemini symbol is pillars, the sign for Leo is the lion, and so on. Both Western and Eastern astrology have symbols for each sign, and we will briefly take a look at both the Chinese and Western systems, the symbols used and their meaning.

WESTERN ASTROLOGY

ARIES

Those familiar with the zodiac system will already be aware that the symbol for Aries is the ram.

The symbol represents the horns of the ram, giving the idea of force, strength, fertility of mind, virility, leadership and masculinity. Also, it should be realised that as Aries is the first sign of the zodiac, tied in with the symbolism is the idea of originality, of the start or the beginning. As some believe that the Earth was created from fire, it is not surprising that the first sign of the zodiac connects with the element of Fire. To the Medo-Persians, the use of the ram with two horns of unequal height as their emblem signified the ascendancy of their power and rulership over lesser nations. To the Egyptians, the ram was a sacred animal, linked with the god Aman-Ra; in Greece it was linked to Zeus, and became symbolic of fertility; to the ancient Israelites, a year-old ram was one of the animals sacrificed yearly for the Passover. Rams were also served as an installation offering for the Aaronic priesthood, and rams were frequently offered as sacrifices – in fact Samuel used 'the fat of rams' to symbolise sacrifice. Rams also represented persons, particularly leaders of nations who, because of their actions, were destined for destruction. In Islam, the ram is still considered the chief sacrificial animal.

It is worthwhile nothing that horns themselves are very symbolic. To ancients, horns were considered to symbolise power, strength and nobility. They were objects for veneration, and many early altars in pagan times had horns placed upon them. The Bible also speaks of 'the horns of the altar', and many ancient illustrations depict men bedecked with horns. In fact, Viking warriors were known to wear horns, and the horn, symbolic of energy – both male and female – is also associated with the horn of plenty or cornucopia, symbolising wealth and plenty. This link comes from the story of Amalthea, a daughter of the King of Crete, who was given the horn by Zeus as a token of appreciation, saying that whoever possessed the horn would never know want. In the East, horns are often found attached to the keys of stables to protect the animals within from harm by evil spirits. This links to the story of the god Pan, who watches over the forests, pastures and flocks, and has the appearance of a goat.

TAURUS

Taurus is symbolised by the bull.

Again horns are an element, but so is the face of the bull. Symbolic of power and of aggression, this stubborn, earthy, reliable and strong animal conveys some of the characteristics of the Taurean person. Once more, links with sacrifices are apparent, and the ritual slaughter of bulls in Spain has seen this idea continue. Bulls themselves are highly complex symbols, sometimes being linked with the Sun and sometimes with the Moon. Many ancient civilisations used the bull in their symbolism, including ancient Egypt, who considered the bull to be one of the most sacred animals, and associated it with death, as did various Asian cultures, although it is worthwhile noting that Carl Jung linked the bull with the father figure, and thus with fertility. In Hinduism, the bull symbolises strength and fertility, and Taurus is an Earth sign, as one would assume from its earthy connections.

GEMINI

Gemini, as we have already seen, in represented by two columns.

Gemini's columns link with duality, with support and with the numbers 11 and 2. Columns, heading as they do towards the heavens, also connect with the element of air, as does the sign of Gemini.

CANCER

Cancer, the fourth sign of the zodiac, is represented by the crab.

Some think this symbol represents the human breasts, and thus has close links with the mother figure, with protection and loving, while others feel it links with the crab's claws, clinging and covert, protective of itself and its delicate interior. As it never seems to move forwards in a straight line, the crab to many is symbolic of those who dodge the truth, and thus is connected with dishonesty.

Looking at the symbol for the crab, however, other people, especially those who study numbers, will immediately see the connection between two number sixes, and thus with the number 12 and all its meanings. Linking with the Moon, and thus with intuition, emotions and passivity, this sign also links with Water.

LEO

Leo is represented, as we have briefly mentioned, by the lion.

The symbol for the lion resembles the mane of the animal, and thus leads one think in terms of leadership, valour, power and strength. Linking with the Sun in planetary terms, this Fire sign is also one of depths, emotions and will.

VIRGO

Virgo is connected with the virgin, and all that this implies.

This symbol represents a woman holding an ear of wheat, considered by many to be a symbol of fertility. It is interesting to note that on many tarot cards for the Empress, there is woman depicted holding bundles of wheat. Connected with Isis, to the Egyptians, and to others with Ishtar, Persephone, Ceres and even with the Virgin Mary, this symbol connects with the number 6, being the sixth sign of the zodiac.

LIBRA

Libra is represented by the scales.

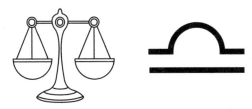

Scales obviously relate to balance, and also to indecisiveness, a strong characteristic of Libra people. Balance and scales generally are symbolic of the balance between spirituality and materialism, with the ego and the subconscious mind, with the balance between physical and mental well-being. Being symbolic since Chaldean times of justice, the scale can also be thought of as a symbol of punishment, or of immanent justice.

SCORPIO

Scorpio is represented by the scorpion and the eagle.

As we have already seen, the eagle has often been connected to the human power, and also to the ability to soar up towards the gods, thus symbolising materialism and spirituality, life and death and the power of the mind. Consequently, the symbol for Scorpio is thought to represent the flight of the human race and its possibility of falling.

The symbol for Scorpio does bear a resemblance to the legs and tail of the scorpion: the scorpion is well known for having a sting in its tail, thus leading to it being a symbol for death and destruction. In early Christian artwork, the scorpion became symbolic of treachery, and was connected to the Jews, whilst to the Mayas it was the sign of the death god, and in fact many ancient civilisations considered the scorpion to be an evil thing. The resulting symbolism behind the sign of Scorpio has lead to thoughts of mysticism, sex, death and rebirth.

SAGITTARIUS

Sagittarius is represented by the centaur with bow and arrow.

The symbol can be seen to show the bow and arrow aimed upwards. Sometimes the sign is shown actually as the centaur (a half man, half horse creature) aiming the arrow, and theories have arisen that this is a combination symbol for heaven and Earth, human and animal, spirit and base instincts. The horse, speed, freedom and restlessness have thus become linked to this zodiac sign.

CAPRICORN

Capricorn is represented by the goat.

 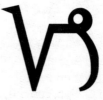

This symbol is a combination of two ideas – the goat and the curling fish's tail, called Capricornus by the Chaldeans. Connecting with the sea, with myth and legend, this sign is now associated with the element of Earth. As the sign stems from two ideas, there is also an element of duality with its symbolism – a tendency towards the depths (of depression perhaps) and the heights of achievement, between the seas and the earth. With its connections with horns, thought by many to represent fertility, Capricorn is also considered to represent fertility in human endeavour, whilst goats generally are symbolic of ceaseless energy.

AQUARIUS

Aquarius is represented by the water carrier.

The symbol for the zodiac sign, being two wavy lines, represents Water, or conversely electricity. Anything connected with water conveys the idea of intuition (as we have already seen with Cancer and its connections). To some, the symbol relates to the flood or deluge, and thus with new beginnings, and this sign, being the first sign at the start of each year, adds weight to this thought. The Egyptians identified Aquarius with Hapi, a god of the Nile, and used a wavy line as a symbol for water. Water has also been symbolic of wisdom, especially to the early civilisations, and of the formation of creation. Being linked to the ceremony of baptism, water is also seen to symbolise resurrection, a new birth and the rebirth of a spiritual person. To students of psychology, water is seen to be symbolic of the birth process and thus fertility. Water can also symbolise destruction, as its power to destroy landmasses is well recorded, and movement, or flow and new ideas.

PISCES

Pisces is the last sign of the western zodiac.

The symbol is representative of two fishes joined together (see the section on Fish in Chapter 2) yet also pulling apart. Connected with Water and also by ancient peoples to Neptune, this symbol means both new cycles and the ending of old ways.

Chinese astrology

Within the Chinese astrology system, we encounter animals, some of which we have already discussed briefly. Students of Chinese astrology will be aware that the start of the Chinese new year, and consequently the dates for each sign within each year vary dependent upon the Moon, and it is worthwhile making sure that you belong to a particular sign before you go on to investigate your characteristics and tendencies. *Chinese Horoscopes for Beginners,* another book in this series, will help you with this. We will not deal here with the characteristics of each zodiac animal, but we will concentrate on its symbolism and meaning throughout the world. Unlike Western Astrology where a graphic symbol is used to represent the sign, in Chinese astrology the animal itself is drawn and its Chinese name written by its side.

RAT

The first sign is the rat, considered a good symbol to the Chinese, although rats to most people are symbolic of disease, death and infirmity. Plagues of rats are well known in history and also in fable – the Pied Piper of Hamlin being one such story. Considered by some to represent fertility, again possibly because of its prolific reproduction, to most the rat is an evil animal. To Hindus, however it is symbolic of prudence, and to the ancient Egyptians, rats were symbolic of wisdom.

OX

The second sign is the ox, considered by the Chinese to be a solid, dependable type, likely to live to a good age. To the Egyptians and Indians the ox is symbolic of sacrifice, such animals often being used for sacrificial purposes. The Greeks and Romans regarded the ox as a symbol of possession, although again it was used as a sacrificial animal. To most, the ox is symbolic of patience, strength, submissiveness and gentleness, and is often connected with the Moon, and thus with darkness. The ox and bull are sometimes interchangeable.

TIGER

The third sign is the tiger, considered brave, compulsive, unrestrained and intense. To the Chinese, it is King of Beasts, whereas a white tiger is one of the celestial emblems, representative of the west. (The other celestial emblems are the dragon for the east, the bird for the south and the tortoise for the north). It also relates to darkness, strength and valour, and to the Eastern countries, it symbolises power. To the ancient Greeks, the tiger symbolised cruelty and anger, whilst to early Christians it represented the defence of order against chaos. Sometimes the tiger is seen in combat with other animals, when it takes on a separate symbolism – for example, should the tiger be depicted in conflict with a reptile, the symbolism is of superiority, but the opposite would apply if the tiger were seen in combat with something larger or with a bird. Quite often, the tiger is symbolic of courage and fierceness.

RABBIT

The fourth sign is the rabbit, traditionally the fertility symbol of the animals. The Chinese also link it to immortality, possibly because of its links with the hare and its connection with the elixir of life. The moon rabbit is prominent in the mid-autumn festivals, but in early Christian artwork, the rabbit is often illustrated at the feet of the Virgin Mary, symbolising victory over passion.

DRAGON

The fifth sign is the dragon, which we have already discussed at length. To most Chinese, the dragon is a benevolent creature, bringer of wealth and good fortune, and is a symbol of authority, being worn on the robes of the imperial family and nobility in past times. Legend suggests that the dragon can make itself invisible when situations suit, and as legend suggests that the dragon can find pearls, it is often depicted surrounded by flames with pearls coming out of its mouth.

SNAKE

The sixth sign is the snake, which we discussed in an earlier chapter. Considered, much as the dragon, to be the guardian of treasure, the snake is a symbol of wisdom.

HORSE

The seventh sign is the horse, a symbol in many differing cultures. It is seen to be affiliated to Mars, as an omen of death (especially if black), and as a symbol of motherhood by Jung. The horse and its speed can also be symbolic of travel and movement, whilst to many Asian civilisations, the horse is symbolic of the universe.

Many early civilisations have gods connected to the horse, and many gods actually are depicted with their horse – Odin is just one of these, whose horse Sleipnir had the runic symbols etched on its teeth. The Trojan horse, used as an offering to Minerva, goddess of wisdom, has led to the horse being considered a symbol of wisdom.

The horse is often depicted in early artwork as pulling the Sun across the sky, and in India it represents Surya, the Sun god, who was also given wings, much like Pegasus, the winged horse. Indian myth also shows Soma, the Moon, as a horse, whilst it is normally seen connecting with the Sun by early civilisations. Its connection with death probably stems from its early use as a sacrificial animal, as it was offered many times to the gods, most often to gods relating to the Sun. It was also sacrificed to Mars because of its use in warfare, and was driven over cliffs to its death in honour of the gods of the sea. Its connection with death has lead to the connection with darkness and with night, hence the word 'nightmare' – it was thought that the horses of the night were responsible for many terrors, and in Scandinavia the chariot of the goddess of the night was drawn across the skies by one horse. Some early Christians felt that the black horse was evil and a form which Satan took when visiting the Earth.

The corn spirit, Demeter, who we have mentioned previously linked with the pentacle and who was also the Corn Mother, was often depicted with a horse's head, having taken this shape to confuse Neptune. The Celtic Corn Mother, Cerridwen, the goddess of inspiration, also has a horse as a symbol, and the goddess Epona was actively portrayed with the horse. Within the British Isles, the horse has always been held in high esteem, and to most peoples it has become a symbol of wisdom. Winged horses, such as Pegasus, symbolise fame, literary skills and swiftness.

GOAT

The eighth sign is the goat. This was discussed fully in the section on the Western sign of Capricorn.

MONKEY

The nineth sign is the monkey, symbolic of the baser side of the human psyche, ever since the Darwinian theories of evolution, perhaps. The monkey is symbolic to the Chinese of good health, success and protection, and is also linked, because of its mischievous ways as having a direct link with fairies, demons, spirits and sprites. Chinese legend also tells of a monkey king, known as Sun Hou-tzu. To early Christians, the monkey symbolised trickery, deception and vanity, and was often linked to Satan.

ROOSTER

The tenth sign is the rooster, symbolic to many as representative of sunset or sunrise; the rooster thus becomes an emblem for the Sun. Sacred to the Greek god Asclepius, the healer and physician, this bird was also seen as an emblem of resurrection, and as it represented the rising of the Sun, it came to symbolise Christ putting to flight the powers of darkness. Active and protective of its territory, the rooster became something embraced by the early Christians as a symbol of protection from evil, and thus appeared regularly on the weather vanes of churches, cathedrals and other religious buildings, turning in all directions to ward off evil. In its guilded form it has obvious symbolic connections with the gold of the Sun, forever shining against the powers of evil. To some ancient civilisations such as the Hebrews, the rooster was symbolic of fertility. In Germany, the rooster is a symbol of the spirit of the corn, and fables tell how it hides in the last sheaf.

DOG

The eleventh sign is the dog, which we have already discussed in an earlier chapter.

PIG

The final and twelfth sign is the pig. Used extensively as a talisman in China, the symbolism of the pig is ancient, it being considered sacred to those who lived in Crete where the god, Jupiter, was said to have been fed by the milk of a pig. Associated with St Anthony in Christian stories, the pig can also be considered a symbol of licentiousness, greed and gluttony, or also of intrepidness, and associations with the wild boar's ability supposedly to be able to smell the wind, leads to it being symbolic of thunder, lightning and rushing winds. Sacred to several cultures, the pig features in many stories: The Three Little Pigs and the romance Journey to the West are Western examples, and legend tells that seven pigs pulled the chariot of Chun T'i, Chinese goddess of light. To many, the term 'pig' is an insult, following on from an ancient Egyptian belief that the pig, especially the black pig, was the home to evil souls. The pig was considered unclean by the Hebrews, and was commonly a sacrificial animal in many countries.

More astrological connections

Before we leave this chapter, we need to consider other astrological connections, and discover the symbols used by astrologers to represent the various planets. Some of the information relates to shapes we have already discussed, but it is necessary to understand a little about astrological symbolism, not just so that we can understand natal charts or astrology, but to see how the symbols relate to others already known to us.

SUN

The main planet in astrology in the Sun. For this reason, many people think of astrology in terms of their Sun sign. It is the placement of the Sun at the date of birth which determines which sign we are born under. The symbol for the Sun, as we have already established, is a circle with a dot at its centre. The circle, symbolising the source, intelligence and spirit, has within it the dot, symbolising the seed of potential contained within the sphere of the universe and of the collective unconscious, and it is not surprising that the ancient Egyptians also associated this symbol with the eye and with the scarab or dung beetle and the phoenix.

As we have established, the worship of the Sun and its various gods and goddesses can be traced way back in our history, and with its ability to shed light and give heat, it is no wonder that the Sun, became a venerated form. Associated with Leo in the zodiac, the Sun is also a card within the major arcana of the tarot. Symbolic of light, of the power of spirit and of glory, it remains constant, unlike the Moon which waxes and wanes, and as such is generally a positive symbol.

MOON

The Moon, with its associations with Cancer the crab, is also connected with the element of Water – tides change with the phases of the Moon. The Moon travels around the Earth and is seen by some to encircle it, and thus the Moon is often symbolic of purity of soul and spirit. Symbolised in astrology as a crescent shape, or incomplete circle, it stands for the evolution of the human spirit, and obviously is connected closely with the half circle, the horseshoe and the rainbow. To ancient Greeks, the Moon was linked to pregnancy, fertility and growth, and thus with the female menstrual cycle. To other ancient civilisations, the Moon was linked with gods and goddesses, in much the same way as the Sun. Generally considered feminine in principle, the Moon was thought, in several cultures, to be the place where the dead lived. Linked to the number 2, the Moon is connected with intuition, and is a potent force within the pagan religions. The pagan Great Moon Goddess is Mother (full Moon), Maiden (crescent Moon) and Wise Woman (waning Moon), and thus is also a trinity. Spells are always performed in conjunction with the phases of the Moon.

MERCURY

Symbolic of communication because of the links with the messenger to the gods, mercury is shown by the symbol below.

Made up of three basic symbols – the half circle, representing the human spirit; the circle, representing the universe and divine spirit; the cross, representing matter and sacrifice – the symbol for Mercury comes directly from the caduceus, which we have already discussed, and is seen to represent intellectual energy, communication and freedom of spirit. Symbolic of soul over spirit over physical matter to the ancient Egyptians, it was also linked to the lizard, itself considered lucky, used to inspire wisdom.

VENUS

Symbolic of unity, feelings of emotion, love and sympathy, Venus is shown by the symbol below:

Formed from the circle and the cross, in biology and medicine this symbol is used for the feminine principle. Connected strongly with love as well as with lust, this is a truly physical symbol, but is also considered to be good, passive and kind. The circle is symbolic of the spirit, whilst the cross is symbolic of matter, and thus the sign concerns the triumph of spirituality over a physical existence.

MARS

Mars, symbolic of aggression, energy, strength and of war due to its links with Mars, the Roman god of war, is shown by the symbol below.

This uses an arrow over the circle, pointing skywards, suggestive of warfare, an object and a direction. This symbol is used within biology and medicine to illustrate the male principle, and its subsequent connection to creation is therefore not surprising. Thought to symbolise the sacrifices we humans make to survive, Mars is normally associated with bloodshed and weaponry, and is the reverse of the symbol for Venus, indicating the struggles of the physical person over the spiritual.

JUPITER

Connected strongly with the eagle, Jupiter is shown by the symbol below.

Composed of a half circle above the horizontal line through which is placed a vertical line, this symbol represents the need for the human spirit to expand and develop, as the soul, represented by the half circle, is seen to be on a level with matter, represented by the horizontal line through which a vertical line has been drawn. Jupiter, the Roman god, was considered one of the most authoritative and powerful of the gods, a protector, guardian and judge, and as lord of the heavens he was always in conflict with the gods of the earth and of the seas. However, his place as one of the most powerful gods has led the symbol of Jupiter to be associated with good judgement and direction.

SATURN

Connected with restrictions and old age, Saturn is shown by the symbol below.

Composed of a vertical line of cross with a half circle, the symbol for Saturn shows that matter is level with soul, and that intuition, coming from the Moon, is linked with the descending of the spirit. The symbol thus emphasises human limitations, the need for order, and the restrictions of time – being closely linked to the god Cronus, also known as Father Time. Sometimes depicted with a scythe, and thus with 'the grim reaper', the symbol became associated with death, through which comes rebirth, and it links, therefore, with the colour black and with tombs, as well as with the sign of Capricorn, coming at the end of the year but moving into the start of the new year. The connection with time also leads to thoughts of movement and restlessness, and so Saturn is also symbolic of activity, of endurance and of reserve. To some, however, Saturn symbolises subjective evil.

URANUS

Uranus, connected with independence and change, is symbolised below.

This symbol is made up of the letter H, because it was discovered by Sir William Hershel in 1781. The use of the circle and the vertical line have led this symbol to be taken abroad by the communications industry, and it has always been seen to be symbolic of the television aerial which it so closely resembles. As Uranus was discovered relatively recently, it symbolises newness, change, movement and discovery, whilst it can also be thought to symbolise matter over spirit but within soul.

NEPTUNE

Neptune is connected with sensitivity, subtlety and refinement. Its symbol is shown below.

The symbol for Neptune relates to the trident the god was said to hold, and thus has strong connections with the number 3. The half circle and cross again are apparent, and this symbol obviously relates heavily to water, but also to anything hidden, as water obviously hides things within its depths, and that also includes emotions, sins and passions. As a result, the symbol signifies the soul descending into the depths of physical form. To many, the trident is a symbol merely of sin.

PLUTO

Pluto, connected with renewal, change and transformation is symbolised in two differing ways.

The symbol above is formed from the initials of Percival Lowell, a prominent astronomer. Pluto was the god of the Underworld, and thus this symbol is often seen to represent death, rebirth and new beginnings.

PLUTO

This alternative symbol for pluto can be thought to represent soul encasing spirit over matter.

COMMON SYMBOLS AND THEIR MEANINGS

*W*e can now move forwards, having learnt about some of the ancient symbols, astrological and planetary symbols and graphic symbols, to take a look at various symbols which may feature in our day-to-day lives. Again, it should be noted that this is not an exhaustive list, as we are not able in the space we have to go through each and every symbol known to the human race. Neither is the list in order of priority. These are but a sample few, some of them follow on from symbolism we have already discussed, and some of them from new thoughts. As we will also see in Chapter 7, some of these symbols link in with the doodles we draw.

EYES

To students of Jungian psychology, the eye is symbolic of the mother's bosom, and the pupil is symbolic of the child. Considered by many to be 'the window to the soul' the eyes will tell us a lot about the emotions; whether a person is sad, happy, concerned, confused and so on. Likewise, eyes can wink, we can shut our eyes when we don't wish to see or face something. Even someone's state of health can be guaged by the appearance of the eyes, especially tiredness. As such it is not surprising that the eye, which allows us to see the things going on around us and also connects to our inner thoughts, has always been a powerful symbol. Considered to be symbolic of intellectual processes and to link with the pineal gland, which is considered by many to be the fountain of psychic powers, the eye was known to the Egyptians as the udjat, wedjat or utchat, connected with the Sun, and the all Sun gods, and if worn as an

amulet was said to protect the wearer's home and family against harm, and bring about good health and prosperity. Used widely as an amulet of magic in Egyptian times, it was generally made from silver or gold, to reflect back 'the evil eye'. Eyes have always been regarded as one of the major tools in understanding, and in spiritual sight, in letting in the light, both actually and metaphorically. The Egyptians particularly illustrated the eye paying huge importance to the placement of the iris in the centre, representative of the Sun, itself giver of light. Plotinus is widely quoted as saying that the eye would not be able to see the Sun if it were not a sun itself.

As the Sun can be seen to heal people, both emotionally and physically, it is not surprising that the eye was also considered by the ancient Egyptians to link with the gods of healing. It also links with Horus, god of the Sun and the sky strongly because it was said that Seth tore an eye from the face of Horus, son of Osiris, during a fight following the death of Osiris who had been killed by Seth. As with many ancient amulets, the Eyes of Horus were often buried with the Egyptian mummies, as it was thought that their sight would guide the dead person through the darkness into the world of Osiris. Known also as the 'all-seeing eye', it is also, with a slight variation, close to the mystical eye in the Great Seal of the USA.

Udjats made of wood were often found as an altar decoration. Eyes feature strongly in many religions. Ancient drawings of Satan often show him having many eyes. In the East, Shiva is illustrated with a third eye placed in the centre of the forehead, symbolising psychic wisdom and clairvoyance, and it is also common to see eyes portrayed in the centre of hands, again symbolic of psychic abilities. As we will shortly see, the eyes also connect with the peacock.

KNOTS

Linked with union, also strongly with anything sexual, and with the tying together of people and beliefs, the knot is a symbol of protection, and not surprisingly also a symbol of true love. To the Chinese, the endless knot is one of the eight emblems of good luck, and is symbolic of long life and happiness. The Egyptian tet, sometimes called the buckle of Isis, was similar in shape and design to the knot in the girdle worn by gods, and was particularly associated with pregnancy and childbirth. A common amulet, normally made out of something red, it was supposed to bring the wearer the virtues of Isis, for it was a representation of the sexual organs of that goddess, as well as being able to give a dead person the power to become a perfect spirit in the next world. When the tet was linked with the djed, or pillar of Osiris, which was quite a common occurrence, this was symbolic of the unconquerable power of Nature.

The knot is often associated with the number 8, and thus with infinity, but also with the thought of being tied down.

ḥANDS

Hands are very important to us: they allow us to pick things up; they allow us to write or type; they allow us the opportunity to touch and link with other people; they allow us to communicate, especially important to those who use sign language as a means of communication; palmists read the lines on the hands to tell us about ourselves. But the hand is also a very powerful symbol in itself. When we shake hands, for example, we are declaring that we have no hidden weapons up our sleeves – these would become dislodged with the shaking process. We also use our hands as a form of greeting – we wave, we raise our hands, the Romans clasped their hand against their breast. Over the centuries hands have become symbolic of protection, authority, strength and power. There are many hands used as symbols in their own right, and hands are also linked with other symbols, birds being one of the most common. A common hand symbol, called The Hand of Fatima, is symbolic of divine power and will protect the wearer against harm. The five digits of the hand themselves are considered to be symbolic of the four limbs of man plus the head. To Bible students, the hand is sometimes symbolic of the self, or of one's general demeanour or action. When linked to God, the hand is symbolic of His power in both creation and destruction. The right hand, particularly, was considered to be of great symbolic importance, possibly because most men were right handed and used the sword in their right hand.

To be on the right hand of a ruler was to have the most important position, next to the ruler himself.

KEYS

Symbolic of life and knowledge, and often seen as the link between the two worlds, the key has always been considered a symbol of good fortune. When people reach maturity, they are often presented with the 'key of the door'. In the Bible, the term 'key' is symbolic of authority, government and power (Peter was told he would receive the keys to the kingdom in Matthew 16:19), and in more recent times in the Middle East, the placing of a key upon a man's shoulder identified him as being a person of authority. The ankh, itself representative of the key, was seen to be the link between the two worlds, and the key has always been symbolic of opening up new areas, and possibly connecting to the unconscious. Often the key is used with other symbols – when linked, for example, with the dove, a creature symbolic of spiritual matters, it is seen to symbolise the opening up of the spirit realms, and thus opening up of knowledge.

LADDERS AND STAIRS

These are symbolic of the climb of the human race ever upwards towards spirituality. In the Bible, there is only one mention of ladders and that appears in Genesis 28:12 in connection with the ladder seen by Jacob in a dream, symbolic of the possibility of communication between heaven and Earth. However, to some, especially those concerned merely with secular interests, the ladder and stairs symbolises the striving of human race ever onwards towards greater achievements, more money, wealth and stability. Stairs relate heavily to the pyramid shape, already discussed in an earlier chapter.

BIRDS

There are many types of birds, and each has its own symbolic meaning: some think the bird is a phallic symbol, others believe it stands for love. In this section, we will take a look at the most common symbolism associated with specific birds, but it is worthwhile noting that to many ancient peoples, birds were considered messengers of the gods, and it is not surprising that the Greeks gave Mercury, their god of communication, winged feet. Often used as a symbol for the soul, birds are considered by the Hindus to be symbolic of higher consciousness. As birds rose up into the sky, it was thought by the Egyptians and other ancient civilisations that they met with the gods, becoming their confidants, and the saying 'A little bird told me' may well have its roots in this thought. Even in early Christian times, it was thought that a flock of birds which flew in the shape of a cross were merely testifying to the fact that Christ had risen, and it is well known that Francis of Assisi regularly preached to both animals and birds. As a result, birds generally are symbolic of the spirit, and can also be seen linked with angels, spirits and supernatural beings. This link between birds and the spirit is very common worldwide, and the bird features in many stories and fables, religions and philosophies. Groups of birds can also be symbolic of thought, of imagination and the need for spirituality. To students of psychology, especially to those familiar with the works of Carl Jung, the bird symbolises spirits, angels, thoughts and flights of fancy.

Owl

The owl is symbolic of wisdom (The Wise Owl) because of its links with the goddess of wisdom, knowledge, education and learning. Said to haunt graveyards, the owl has also become symbolic of death and the night, possibly because of its connection with Athene, goddess of wisdom, who was also at one time goddess of the night, and stories have been written to suggest that the owl, as well as the raven, are omens of death. Many cultures feel that the owl is symbolic of evil, including those of China and Japan. Biblical mentions of the owl connect it to blindness and ruin and with being unclean. To the Hebrews, it was considered an unclean bird, whilst early Christians generally associated it with Satan and with Evil, possibly following on from an earlier pagan superstition. Seeing an owl during the daytime is considered an especially bad omen.

SWAN

The swan is symbolic of purity, due to its pure white colouring, and links with the elements of Air and Water, but also is thought by some to link with the Sun. It is symbolic of divinity due to its links with Zeus who visited Leda in the shape of a swan. Hindu mythology suggests that a swan laid the cosmic egg from which Brahma emerged. Early Celtic peoples used the skin and feathers of the swan to make ceremonial cloaks for the poet, leading the swan to become a symbol of language. It is connected to magic, and it was listed as one of the unclean flying creatures in Hebrew literature.

SWALLOW

The swallow is symbolic of good luck, hope and improving conditions, probably due to its arrival at Spring, and is a bringer of good fortune, especially on the domestic front. Linked to Isis, Venus and Aphrodite, swallows were caught by ancient Greek women, who smeared them with oil and then released them, which represented the leaving of the house of any bad omens. To Christians, the swallow is symbolic of new life and the resurrection, and Moslems also consider it a sacred symbol. To the Chinese, it is symbolic of success, even in the face of adversity.

STORK

Storks have always been a symbol of new birth, and are linked to Juno by the Romans. Their connection with babies comes from the story that the stork found the embryos of Mother Earth whilst fishing in the creative waters. Also symbolic of travel, the stork is often shown flying with a new baby in his beak. To the early Christians, the stork was symbolic of purity and of faithfulness, as it is known to be faithful all its lifetime to one mate. Its connections with babies and the starting out of life connected it to Christ and to the new personality which Christians adopted when leaving behind their previous thoughts and actions.

WOODPECKER

Woodpeckers have long been linked to the tree and considered to be its protector, but to Christians, the woodpecker is symbolic of Satan, pecking away at the Tree of Life and undermining the belief of the people.

Ostrich

The Ostrich to many symbolises an inability to face up to reality, by virtue of the fact that the ostrich is seen to bury its head in the sand. However, the ostrich is also symbolic of truth and justice, and linked to the goddess Maat. Considered to be a divine bird by the Zoroastrians, and as a symbol of creation, life and resurrection by many other religious movements, the ostrich is often used in heraldry, normally depicted with items in its beak.

Wren

The wren is sometimes used in place of the dove to represent the spirit, but to some it is seen as representative of witchcraft. Considered a lucky omen in Japan, it is symbolic of good fortune and a pleasant future. Actively tracked down and killed as part of a Christmas festival in France, the bird's death was seen as symbolic of the end of the year and the start of the next.

Pelican

Pelicans, originally one of the unclean birds listed in the Mosaic Law of the Hebrews, became a symbol for Christ, due to the bird's habit of pecking its breast until it bleeds and then feeding its young with the blood. Obviously this shows an element of self-sacrifice, and ties in with the sacrifice of Christ for us, and with the giving of His blood in order that we might live. As a result, the pelican is considered a symbol of altruistic love and devotion. This may be the reason why, along with the eagle, the pelican is used as part of the decoration on church lecturns. However, to the Hebrews, the bird was considered unclean and symbolic of ruin (Psalms 102:6), and in the Bible it is generally used to symbolise desolation (Isaiah 34:11, Zephaniah 2:13 and 14). This probably stems from its preference to live in uncultivated areas where humans cannot disturb it. The pelican is also one of the principal symbols in alchemy.

Peacock

The peacock, with its splendid colours, is symbolic of incorruptibility, possibly because its colours associate with matters regal, and also to totality, because all the colours blend in to form the tail feathers. It is recorded how King Solomon's ships regularly brought back various treasures from their voyages, including peacocks. Linked with the Ming Dynasty by the Chinese, and often used in artwork by ancient civilisations, the peacock was a symbol of the emperor to the Romans, whilst to the Hindus, it is sacred to Kema, god of love, and Veda Sarasvati, goddess of music and wisdom. The peacock was sacred to the bird-god Phaon to the ancient Greeks, and was linked with Isis by the Egyptians. Legend suggested that the tail of the peacock contained the eyes of Argus, blinded by the goddess Hera, and because of their watchfulness, peacocks are said to ward off evil, and are often kept in the grounds of temples. However, it is worthwhile remembering that even Argus, with all his eyes, could not escape death. This fact seems to have been ignored by the early Christian Church, who used the peacock actively as a symbol of immortality, resurrection and, with reference to the tail feathers which can be likened to eyes, with the 'all-seeing' Church. To Buddhists, the peacock is symbolic of compassion, marital fidelity and watchfulness, whilst to followers of Islam, the peacock represents the eye of the heart.

Kingfisher

The kingfisher, another bird with wonderful colours, also known as the Halcyon, is associated with calm and beauty, particularly by the Chinese. As it is a shy and retiring bird, not often seen, it is also symbolic of a modest person with a shy and retiring character.

Robin

The robin, associated in many countries with Christmas and its festivities was once symbolic of death, possibly because its appearance at the end of the year heralds the death of that year, but it is also worth remembering that it also heralds the start of the next. It is said that the robin got its red breast by attempting to remove the nails from Christ's body after the crucifixion, and as such it was a foregone conclusion that it would be used heavily in the Christian Yuletide celebrations. Early symbolism linked the robin to Fire, and this link is echoed in Scandinavia, where it is sacred to Thor, the god of fire and thunder.

RAVEN

The raven is associated with death, and also with warfare, but as a Christian symbol, it is linked to Satan and evil, possibly because it has links with the pagan Bran the Blessed, Bran meaning raven. Considered a symbol of evil by the ancient Egyptians and the Hebrews, it is the first bird actually mentioned in the Hebrew Scriptures at Genesis 8:7, and was seen to be symbolic of ruin and desolation. Declared unclean by the Hebrews, it also one of the birds used by God to carry bread and meat twice a day to Elijah whilst he was hiding in the valley of Cherith (1 Kings 17:2–6). Devoted to its young and known to have the same mate for life, the raven has connections with various gods, including the Norse god Odin, who had two ravens called Hugin (Thought) and Munin (Memory) which he sent around the world to act as his spies and report back. As such, the raven became symbolic of help and protection, especially to gods and those engaged in battles. To the ancient Greeks, the raven was a prophetic bird, whilst to other ancient peoples, it was considered an omen of death. The raven was sacred to the god Apollo, and to the early British, it was the shape in which Morrigham appears over the battlefields with her family, and there are many stories of the raven-women in Arthurian legend. To the Chinese and the Greeks the raven was connected with the Sun, and it is thought to be symbolic of power by many cultures. It is said that when the ravens leave the Tower of London, the British monarchy will fall, and for this reason the wings of the birds are kept clipped. This legend could link with the Celtic god Bran, who is thought to have been buried on Tower Hill to ward off invaders.

VULTURE

Vultures, because of their habit of scavenging, are symbolic of goodness, in as much as they clear the Earth of rot and decay,

especially important in hot countries where putrefying flesh might otherwise cause disease. To some, especially the Parsees, this is thought to speed up the process of rebirth. Sacred to the goddess Isis, who once took the form of a vulture, these birds are also symbolic of maternal care and thus are symbolic of the mother, although early thoughts were that the vulture was a destructive bird. Another bird considered unclean by the Hebrews, the vulture is still considered the foulest of scavengers in the Middle East.

FLOWERS

There are many symbols connected with flowers, and also many myths. Sunflowers, for example, because of their bright yellow colour were linked to the Sun, and were consequently thought to have magical properties, strengthen the mind and bring about an abundance of energy. Another such myth is that flowers should be removed from a sickroom at night. When asked why it is necessary to do this, some people will suggest that the flowers will take away extra oxygen which may be needed, but the truth of the matter is that it was originally felt that evil spirits hid in the petals of flowers during the daylight hours, to emerge at night and attack the patient while he or she slept. The mimosa was for many centuries thought to help ward off evil spirits, and was hung above the beds of those who were ill, but sometimes even this was removed from the sickroom because it was felt that it could induce psychic dreams, which could prove to be dangerous if not properly understood.

Rose

Linked with Venus, Aphrodite, Ishtar and Isis , and thus with love, the rose became associated with virginity, martyrdom, the search for perfection and spirituality and the heart, considered to be the most important organ by most cultures. It is interesting to note that originally the symbol of love was the red tulip, but this linkage dwindled and the rose symbol became more and more prominent. Only in certain countries has the red tulip held its links as a symbol of love.

A single rose is considered to be a symbol of completion and perfection, and possibly the tradition of presenting one's love with a single red rose brings into play the thoughts of both love and the idea that the object of desire is perfect.

Qabalists link the rose to Tiphareth, where it is symbolic of harmony and beauty, and its links with ancient religions and traditions led it to be shunned by the early Christian Church. However, Christendom eventually bowed under pressure and linked the rose to the Virgin Mary, and the rosary's beads were once made from rose petals. Following on from the rose's acceptance within the Christian Church, rose windows became popular, and these can be found in many churches and cathedrals. Because the shape of the rose resembles the mandala, especially when it is in full bloom, it was felt at one time that looking at a rose window could bring about a meditative state. Another popular thought is that placing a bag of rose petals under the pillow at night time will lead to dreams of a future lover or spouse.

Legends which include the rose are many. One such tells that whilst rushing to be at the side of her dying lover, a god cut her foot open on some rose briars. The blood she shed dyed the white roses red, and thus the rose became associated both with love and with death. Many people still refuse to have white and red flowers in the same vase, considering them symbolic of blood and bandages, and also therefore of death.

Used often as part of ceiling decoration, the white rose was said to have been given to Harpocrates, god of silence, by Eros in an attempt to persuade him to keep silent about the goddess Venus's love affairs. As a result it is considered to be a flower of secrecy, and thus its useage on ceilings symbolised the idea that things mentioned in that room would not be divulged elsewhere. This idea was transferred to the use of the rose as a sign outside taverns and public houses, and it is well recorded that in Roman times, the sign of a rose outside such a place signified that anything said inside, whether in a state of sobriety or drunkenness, would remain confidential.

In English history there are many links with the rose, and it is well documented how the English houses of York (red rose) and

Lancaster (white rose) used this flower as their symbol. Following the Wars of the Roses, the Rose of England or Tudor Rose became symbolic of the linking of the two houses, although it is interesting to note that the rose normally has five petals, thus linking it with the number of Mars, and thus with warfare.

Many organisations and people have used the rose as an emblem. Akhnaton, an Egyptian pharoah had the cross and the rose as symbolic of brotherhood; Andreae's family crest was a cross of St Andrew with four roses between the arms; that of Martin Luther was a rose with a cross in the centre.

Often the amount of petals the rose has is significant. The eight-petalled rose, for example, is symbolic of regeneration, whilst the rose with seven petals is symbolic of perfection, linking in with the seven days of the week, the seven Ages of Man, the seven planets, etc.

Used as a symbol together with the cross by the Rosicrucians, the twenty-two-petalled rose is symbolic of the Order of the Golden Dawn.

The Romans were particularly fond of planting white and red roses on tombs of dead lovers. White roses are thought to be symbolic of modesty, whilst red roses symbolise passion and desire. As a result, the sending of red roses to a loved one is quite apt. Pink, considered to be the colour of unconditional love, leads to many sending pink roses to their loved ones, whilst others, linking the colour yellow both to wisdom, achievement and to love, will choose to send their lovers yellow roses. The blue rose is said to be a symbol of the impossible. For those interested in an astrological link, the rose flower actually belongs to Taurus.

NARCISSUS

The narcissus links with the Greek legend of the young man of the same name who was told he would have a happy life unless he saw his image reflected. Catching sight of himself in the waters of a stream, it is said he fell desperately in love with himself, and unable to move from the spot, slowly died. As such the narcissus links with love, both of self and of others, and the enrichment of relationships, both old and new. It also links with contemplation, with a self-sufficient attitude and with self-absorbency.

IRIS

The iris is another flower which is a symbol of love, and in some parts of the USA its root is sprinkled on to the sheets of a bed in order to bring about passionate feelings. It is also said to help form a link between the conscious and unconscious mind.

JASMINE

The jasmine is a sacred flower to the Chinese, and is said to be a symbol of femininity and purity, and to bring about feelings of physical attraction and sensuality. Thought to help men be more open about their feelings and attract someone new into their lives, it is also thought to help boost self-esteem, and as such is often found in bridal bouquets.

DEVIL OR SATAN

An obvious symbol of evil, this is one of the cards within the major arcana section of the tarot. Mostly portrayed as having a human torso but the legs of a goat, the devil symbol is linked to all things hidden, to the water and the depths, to the Underworld and thus to Fire, and also to the baser human instincts, and to demons whose main purpose is to lead us astray. As a result, Satan is also symbolic of materialism, of anything relating to falsehood, corruptibility, greed, averace, etc. Often used as a symbol of many temptations faced during one's lifetime, the devil can be portrayed with or without horns, a subject we have already discussed. He can also be portrayed as having many eyes, again as previously mentioned.

HEART

An obvious romantic symbol, the heart is also a central organ in the body. Without the heart beating, we would not live, and it was therefore considered by the ancient Egyptians to be the seat of the

soul and intelligence, as well as the seat of affection, and the place where all memory and knowledge were stored. Symbolic of protection and true love, the ib or heart was the only major organ not to be removed in mummification. The Egyptian *Book of the Dead* has illustrations of the deceased person's heart being weighed on the scales against the ostrich feather of right and truth, in order to guage the spiritual weight of the person, and find out whether that person had led a life free from sin.

Connected closely with the centre, and thus with the circle and anything circular, including the Sun and other planets, the heart has long been symbolic of light, love and happiness.

cup, goblet or chalice

Linked to Nephthys in ancient Egyptian times, the cup became the symbol of things hidden, contained and yet revealed, and as such was linked to tranquillity. This symbolism is still widely accepted by many. As students of the tarot will know, the suit of cups is one of the suits of the minor arcarna, and is symbolic of anything emotional, with relationships and with love and marriage. Often at special occasions, especially weddings, toasts are made to the happy couple, and the cup or glass raised, possibly aluding to the idea of the cup symbolising a happy relationship. Chalices are often used in Christian tradition, where it is thought by some to hark back to the Holy Grail, symbolic of both spirituality and the Earth. Linked with the cauldron, and thus to witchcraft and paganism, the goblet complete with lid was, to the Romans, a symbol of the human heart.

spider

Sacred to the god Mercury, the spider is a busy creature weaving its web, and as such it is a symbol for good business sense and foresight especially in business situations. Creative with its weaving, the spider has also become a symbol of creativity, and is linked with the Great Mother, to whom we are tied when born by the umbilical cord. This weaving has led the spider to be highly respected in Hinduism and Buddhism where it is symbolic of the weaving of illusion. The spider's habit of weaving its web in a circular fashion converging on a focal point in the centre has led it to have connections with the spiral shape, which we have already discussed. There are only two mentions of spiders in the Bible – at Job 8:14 where apostates are linked to those who lean on a spider's house, something obviously too frail to support them, and at Isaiah 59:5, where the actions of the unfaithful Israelites are linked to the weaving of a spider's web. Many ancient peoples thought that the spider related to the Moon, and thus to the night, and therefore it can also be symbolic of death. Christianity has taken the spider to be symbolic of cunning, by the way in which it catches its prey in its web, and thus it followed on that the spider and its web became symbolic of Satan, who seeks to trap the unsuspecting sinner. Possibly because of this connection with Satan, the spider also became associated with the love of money and materialism.

Lotus

Illustrated in many cultures as the emergence of light from darkness, the lotus to the ancient Egyptians represented the possibility of enlightenment for humanity, and it was said that at the moment of creation, a lotus bud rose to the surface of the waters, opened its petals and Horus then spread the rays of the Sun across the Earth. It is the original water lily, fleur-de-lis or flower of light, signifying birth, rebirth and resurrection, and was linked with the heart in the Middle Ages especially. As a result, to many the lotus is a symbol of evolution and progression, whilst it can also be thought to be one of the flowers of love and of sexual concerns, the pink lotus especially being symbolic of the female reproductive organs. To the Egyptians, however, if the lotus and the bull were depicted side by side, the symbol was associated with the Sun gods, whereas when the lotus was linked with a cow, the association was with the Moon goddesses. As it was thought that the lotus's roots began deep down in the depths, grew upwards and then flowered, the root became symbolic of the umbilical cord and human origins, the flowers represented the rays of the Sun and the seed pod was the flower to the seeds of creation. Blue lotus designs were particularly popular in

Egypt for many years, where the blue lotus was associated with the Nile and therefore also with fertility.

The lotus is sacred as a symbol to Hindus and Buddhists: the Hindus consider it a symbol of non-attachment to the material world – being in the world but not a part of it, just as the lotus floats on the water and remains dry. In India, the crown chakra is depicted by the thousand-petalled lotus, or sometimes lily, and it is therefore linked with the wheel and with circular symbolism. The lotus is often depicted growing from the navel of Vishnu, symbolising the universe with the Sun as its central point, and as such connecting with the Hindu creation stories. To Buddhists, the lotus is symbolic of true human nature, and the seven-petalled lotus appears both in Buddhist and Hindu stories. It was said that eating a lotus made one content and happy, and as such the stories of the lotus-eaters who lived on the Libyan coast became popular.

BOATS AND SHIPS

Both boats and ships are vehicles in which people can travel and items can be carried. As such, especially in the field of psychology, both boats and ships link to pregnancy. Ships also link with travel and obviously with navigation across oceans, and as such they link with the travels of early Christians, especially Paul. Thus they became a symbol for the Church, especially in early times.

MIRROR

The main symbolic meaning behind the mirror is one of reflection. Linking with the symbol of water, with the story of Narcissus and with contemplation, the mirror also symbolises the memories, the unconscious mind and the imagination and has long been considered to link with the Moon, possibly because the Moon's reflection can be seen easily at night upon water. Sacred to Hathor, goddess of nourishment (linked to the nourishing cow), of strength (through its connections with the lion) and provisions, the mirror became linked to anything involving women, from culinary things through to romance and affection. It was felt to be a possible entrance to another world, and this thought possibly influenced the writing of *Alice Through the Looking Glass*.

houses and castles

Various ideas on the symbolic meaning behind these buildings have been levied over the centuries. Psychologists look on the house or castle as representative of outward appearances. The more floors the home appears to have, the more levels there are to explore. Houses or castles with moats or which appear on top of a hill are symbolic of a need for privacy and seclusion, of protection and enclosure, whereas those with a dungeon or cellar are symbolic of hidden depths and unconscious desires. Castles are particularly associated with legends and their inhabitants with either good or evil, dependent upon which story you happen to be reading at the time. Many castles seemed to be occupied by wicked people who kept others imprisoned in the tower. In stories where the princess or maiden manages to effect an escape, it is felt the symbolism lies with the underlying theme that one can escape from evil, given the right circumstances and by grasping the opportunities.

Stairs obviously link each element of our psyche to the other, and differing types of staircase are felt to symbolise differing types of personality. We will see in Chapter 6 how houses and castles can be used in meditation as an aid to understanding our inner selves.

weapons

In most stories and fables, the person who wins against the monster or foe is the person with the weapon. Consequently, weapons are symbolic of power, destruction, battle and struggle. They have a huge phallic significance, and can be symbolic of the struggle of the individual with his or her own sexuality and passion, or conversely with the powers of evil and/or materialism. Many tales and stories tell of the person with the sword, hammer, slingshot, rod, spear, trident or whatever fighting against the dragon or other such creature, or even in the case of David and Goliath against another

being. The person with the weapon invariably wins through in the end, even if after a struggle. As such, weapons tend to be symbolic of the fact that, whatever the battle, we can win through in the end.

TREES

One of the most fundamental symbols in every civilisation and in most religious beliefs is that of the tree. Symbolically standing for immortality and eternity, the tree features in religions as diverse as Christianity and paganism. Most countries have sacred links with trees, and the variety of trees is immense. As such the tree is a global symbol, albeit with slight differences in interpretation.

Considered to have been at the centre of belief by many religions, Christianity being only one of these, the tree became symbolic of the world itself and its links with higher spiritual forms and beliefs. In the Bible, we are told that there were two trees in the Garden of Eden – the Tree of Knowledge of Good and Bad and the Tree of Life, which stood in the middle of the garden. It was from the Tree of Knowledge of Good and Bad that Eve, persuaded by the serpent, ate from, and thus sin was born into the world. Much has subsequently been written about the Tree of Life and why it was not also mentioned as forbidden to Adam and Eve, and many hypotheses have come about, usually assuming that the Tree of Life was, in fact, hidden. Many civilisations make mention of two trees in the formation of the world, and it is suggested that these are symbolic of good and evil and human duality – physical and spiritual. In many ancient illustrations, the Tree of Life is illustrated upside down – the roots are in heaven and the leaves on the Earth. In Norse tradition, the Tree of Life or Tree of the World is called Yggdrasil, and is an ash tree, which is normally illustrated in 'accepted form', with its roots being thought to go down into the Underworld. It was said that Yggdrasil will fall with the final battle of Ragnarok at the end of time, when the gods and the forest giants will fight and the whole of creation will be involved. This will end with fire and with death, with the righteous gods going off to the highest of heavens and the evil ones being cast down into Nastrond, the Norse equivalent of hellfire.

Trees are considered to be both feminine and masculine, and as such the thought of duality is perpetuated. In addition, many other symbols are seen to relate to the tree – snakes, dragons and so on, forming their own connections.

In Qabalistic teachings, the Tree of Life is a primary image for meditation, and is symbolic of the path that we can take to reach spirituality and wisdom. Each sephirot or path is a level of knowledge which can be attained, with ten such paths being immediately obvious, linking to the number of completion, but with twenty-two paths being possible. Each sephirot comprises the name of God, the Tetragrammaton. If you are interested in the Qabalah, you should read *Quabalah – a beginner's guide*, in this series, especially if you wish to proceed with meditations linked to the Tree of Life.

LABYRINTH AND MAZE

Once inside a maze or labyrinth, it is sometimes difficult or seemingly impossible to find the way out. From this basic realisation comes the symbolic meaning of the maze as being something from which it is difficult to escape, and something remote and unconquerable. There were many labyrinths in the ancient worlds, both in Europe and Asia. The word labyrinth actually comes from the Cretan word labrys, which was a double axe and an important religious symbol to the ancient peoples of Crete. Those who have visited the Temple of Knossos in Crete may already know the story of the place. Built by Daedalus as a prison for the minotaur, there was only one entrance which led down winding corridors, many with dead ends. Theseus managed to find his way through the labyrinth successfully, killed the minotaur and also managed to find his way out again, with the help of Ariadne's thread. Stories of the construction of a labyrinth being intended to trap demons are well known, but the principles behind the labyrinth and the symbolism involved are very much tied in with the symbolism of the spiral, and also with dance which we have already discussed. Psychologists would suggest that the maze is symbolic of the realisation that we have lost our

spirituality with the progress the human race has made, whilst others connect the labyrinth and cross with the wisdom of God.

Once we have managed to find our way out of the maze, we will have succeeded in conquering evil – much the same really as the ideas concerning weaponry.

6

thinking of meditation

In the course of this book, we have covered a lot of information on various signs and symbols which exist in our world and in that of our ancestors. We have looked at the roots of many of these symbols, discussed their meanings in varying parts of the globe and also the symbolic meaning that many within the field of psychology now place on them.

In this chapter, we are going to take a brief look at how symbolism can be used in meditation. I would like to emphasise that this book is not about meditation but about symbolism, and as such we will be able to give only the briefest information on the correct way to develop meditation as a useful part of everyday life. There are many books which can help you with learning the art of relaxation, visualisation and meditation, and I would recommend that you consider Meditation for Beginners, Visualisation for Beginners *and* Spiritual Healing – a beginner's guide *all books in this series. These will provide a useful starting point for those who are unfamiliar with meditation, visualisation and the healing benefits involved.*

Relaxation

Before we are able to even think about meditation, we must be fully relaxed. Today, this is sometimes an insurmountable problem in itself, with many of us working perpetually on overdrive, unable to switch off or spend time with our families, let alone relax.

From a health angle, it is really important that we do learn to relax, and I would suggest that we all try to find at least fifteen minutes during each day when we can unwind.

There are varying suggestions as to the best time to relax. Some people would suggest that relaxing during the morning will help to set us up for the day, whilst others feel that relaxation is something which should be done after the daily work has been undertaken. I would stress here that by relaxation I really don't mean sitting in front of the TV, listening to news programmes or reading the newspaper or even a good book. All these things are forms of unwinding but lead us to lose ourselves in another form. To be truly relaxed, and especially to meditate, we need to be totally free from distractions and, preferably, other people.

If we can take ourselves off to a room where we won't be interrupted, possibly also take the telephone off the hook, or choose a time when the rest of the household is out, we can start to work on relaxing. Some people prefer to relax and meditate sitting down. There are various poses which different meditation groups will suggest, but I personally feel that sitting in a chair with arms and legs uncrossed is by far the best method. By sitting in this position, our bodily energies, our *ch'i* or *prana*, can flow unhindered. Likewise, our blood flow will also be unhindered, and we are unlikely to get cramps and, especially if we suffer with arthritis or any other joint problem, we are also unlikely to find ourselves in pain, which itself will completely ruin any thoughts of relaxation or of meditation.

To start to relax we need to learn how to breathe. We breathe naturally, but often don't breathe properly, and our lungs are seldom used to their fullest capacity. Women, especially, tend to be shallow breathers by that I mean that we tend to let our chest rise and fall and keep our abdomen still. This is probably a cosmetic thing, as we don't wish to draw attention to our stomach areas, which, for many of us, aren't as flat as we would like. There is absolutely nothing wrong with allowing our lungs to fill completely with oxygen. By taking deep breaths, in through our nose and out through our mouth, holding the breath for around five seconds per time, we will start to relax our muscles. I always suggest to people that when they breathe in through their noses, they imagine that they are breathing in a lovely fragrance, something which they like, and that when they blow out, they imagine that they are blowing at the flame of a candle, but not with sufficient force to blow it out, but merely trying, as many children do, to get the flame to flicker slightly.

Many people may experience a feeling of light-headedness by doing this, and I would stress that this isn't anything to worry about. It is merely the fact that the body hasn't been used to getting so much oxygen at any one time before. After practice and time, the body will get used to the influx of oxygen and the light-headed feelings will subside and eventually disappear. For some people, it is also necessary to progressively tense and relax every muscle group, starting with the feet and working upwards to the face and head, in order to fully ensure that we are totally relaxed. This in itself helps us to focus our minds on our bodies and the tension and stress contained within it, and also helps to block out other thoughts. If you personally wish to try the muscle relaxing routine, start with your toes, clench them up, and then relax them. Adopt a similar practice all the way up your legs, contracting the muscles and then relaxing them. Don't forget to include your hands, your stomach and especially your shoulders: much tension is locked within the shoulder and neck area, as those who have been for massages will no doubt be aware. We often don't realise just how tense we are, and the progressive contracting and releasing of the muscles will often prove a revelation in itself.

In order to begin to think about meditation, we need to be able to clear our minds of day-to-day things. This can be a difficult exercise, and something which takes a lot of effort to master correctly. Those people who aren't able to reach the state of relaxation easily shouldn't be dissuaded to continue, but should realise that, perhaps, relaxation and meditation are, to them, more important than they previously thought.

USING SYMBOLS

When in a totally relaxed state, we can start actively using symbols to help us to achieve or maintain a meditative state. It is important that whatever symbol we choose, it is one with which we feel happy and content. It is absolutely no use my suggesting that you use, let's

say, a candle's flame, if you have a fear of fire. Some people, especially those with strong religious convictions, use a symbol of their own religion. Jewish people or whose interested in the Jewish tradition could try thinking of a star, especially the Star of David or the Seal of Solomon which we have already discussed, and so on. Many people, and I will admit to being one, actively use the symbol of the rose. I feel happy with that symbol, and as I consider that the colour pink is one of unconditional love, a thought echoed by many other people, I try to concentrate my mind on a beautiful pink rose. With my eyes shut, but not squeezed too tightly shut, I visualise the rose. Some people, especially those who are new to the art of meditation and visualisation may need to actively have in front of them the object that have chosen. If this applies to you, make every effort to find an object which is pertinent to meditation, and something with which you feel happy.

If you do have such an object, look at it carefully. If you are able to visualise the item without its physical presence, all well and good. I try to think of my rose's beauty, of its smell and the wonder of its creation. Sometimes in order to be able to visualise the rose, I see it as part of a group of roses decorating the doorway to a cottage, or sometimes even actively seek to recall the times when I have been given such a rose by a friend or loved-one. I think about the rose as a bud, think how its petals are so tightly closed together. Often, as the meditation progresses, and as I relax more and more into the meditative state, the rose will open its petals, to reveal its centre. I look at the rose in its entirety, from its stem right up to its petals and leaves. As I meditate, I tend to link this rose with my heart and in particular with my heart chakra, allowing the colour of the rose and the symbolism behind it to permeate my very being, filling me with love and contentment. I feel that the colour and symbolism behind the rose has actually gone into my body through my skin's pores, through each and every breath I have taken. It has passed into my bloodstream and travelled throughout the whole of my body, filling me with the power of love and happiness.

It is important to try to stay in this meditative and relaxed state for around fifteen minutes. Whatever you do, don't think of having anything in the room which will make a noise after that time has elapsed. If you stay in that state for a little longer or a little less than fifteen minutes, that's fine. You need to come out of the meditative state gradually. A sudden re-emergence into the everyday world is not a good idea. Gradually increase your breathing to a normal rate, and open your eyes gradually and slowly. You may find that the light will hit you and you won't be able to see too well, and for this reason many choose to draw the curtains in the room to help, not only with the relaxation process, but also with the 'coming around' from the meditative state.

There are many flower symbols which you might like to consider other than the rose, especially if you are happy with the concept of flowers. One of the most popular symbols, especially to those with Eastern learnings, is that of the lotus, which we have already discussed as symbolic of enlightenment. Many of us don't have access to a lotus flower, or may never have seen one. If that applies to you, try to think of a water-lily, as they are from the same family. If you wish to, you may even think of the flower on the top of water, should you feel happy with water as a concept. You might wish to visualise not only the flower itself, but also its roots. Think how deep they go beneath the surface; think how the flower grows up from such muddy depths to reach the light, and as you progress in this visualisation, realise that this is echoing your mind and your spirituality, reaching ever upwards from the depths of materialism and the everyday world towards a state of total enlightenment, spirituality and happiness.

Using a mandala for meditation

In an earlier chapter, we mentioned the mandala. This is a form often used by those who practise the art of meditation, and is something which you may wish to try to use from the outset. The circle, as we have established, has no beginning and no end, and is this representative or eternity. It is a shape which has an outside

and an inside, and thus is symbolic of protection and enclosure. Inside the circle of the mandala are other shapes and symbols.

If you wish to draw a mandala, you must start with a circular shape. You can then draw in any other graphics with which you feel comfortable. I have used a mandala in relaxation and meditation, and in order to find a shape with which I felt happy, I bought a child's kaleidoscope. I sat for some time with this, going through the many patterns which it can make, until I found something which I liked. I sought to draw and to colour in the shape I had decided upon. This in itself took some time. The colouring is most important, as colours themselves can be symbolic. If you have used colour in healing, for example, you will already know this. Many have suggested that red, orange and yellow are good colours, possibly because they are quite traditional. I don't necessarily believe that this is a rule which needs to be followed. I prefer purple, indigo and blue to anything red or vibrant, feeling that red is symbolic of passion and of energy, and thus conflicts with the feeling which it is hoped to achieve. However, I leave it with you to make up your own mind. If you are familiar with the chakra centres and actively aware of problems with a particular chakra you may wish to use the colours associated with that chakra, but again it is purely a personal choice, and you really must feel happy with whatever colours and forms you use. After all, meditation really is the ultimate personal experience, and it isn't right for anybody to lay down hard and fast rules for someone else.

When using a mandala, you may wish to sit and look at your drawing or graphics for some time, familiarising yourself with each and every part of it before allowing yourself to shut your eyes and meditate. Again, each of us is different, and it is up to the individual to find the best path for him or herself.

Taking a Mental Journey

Many times during a meditation, and especially when I am leading meditation sessions for other people, I use a variety of symbols and lead the person or group through a series of stages. There are two such guided imageries which I actively use, one of which can be found in *Spiritual Healing – a beginner's guide*. This actively concerns problems and the removal of problems during a meditative state. If you feel that this is a meditation which you can use to effect, please give it a try, as many people, myself included, have benefited from its use. Often it helps those people new to meditation to master the visualisation process. Having a series of visualisations and symbols is often easier for newcomers to grasp than one symbol or image from which their mind can wander. Using a guided imagery, you have a series of symbols, and if they are linked together to form a continuous theme, this can be a very rewarding meditation.

VISUALISATION PRACTICE 1

When in a relaxed state, imagine that you can see a brick wall. That brick wall is painted white. You can see each brick and you can see only the wall, nothing else is visible. Imagine that you see a small hole in that brick wall. It is only a very small hole, but you approach it, and look through it to see what lies beyond. You can see a field. You really like the look of the field, and want to be there, rather than stuck behind the brick wall. You decide to try to enlarge the hole in the wall in order to create a space big enough for you to climb through. Little by little, you take away the cement, mortar and bricks. This takes time. You may not find yourself able to get through the hole at the first attempt. You might find that you can, however, get through the hole by the end of the first session. As I said before, we are all different. If you are lucky enough to be able to get through the hole, you will find yourself in the field. Everything there is perfect. It is a paradise. The wall is behind you. You are somewhere warm, you feel happy, relaxed and at peace with yourself and the world around you. You have no need to return to the wall and the feelings you had when behind it. Stay in that visualisation for as long as you can before coming back to 'the real world'.

The wall has been used in this meditation as a symbol of our problems or of an illness that we might have, or our state of mind. By breaking through the wall, we have left our problems behind us, found happiness and contentment.

Another symbolic journey which I have used to good effect, concerns the use of houses, castles and homes. This is a particularly good symbol to use for most people, as everybody has their own particular idea of their ideal home or dwelling. It can also be quite interesting from an analytical standpoint, finding out, especially from a group, what types of buildings they saw and what was inside. For those of you who wish to try this, you may find it helps to record the visualisation below, so that you can listen to the tape, leading yourself through the various processes as a starting point. For those who are well practised in the art of meditation and guided imagery, the exercise will be fairly easy to follow when you have read the outline. I would suggest, however, that you keep a pen and paper by your side, and write down as many details as you can possibly remember about the meditation *after* the event.

VISUALISATION PRACTICE 2

You are standing before a house. It has a drive leading up to it, and gates at the head of the drive. You stand behind the gates and look up towards the house. Slowly, you open the gates and take a walk up the drive. Look at what you see as you walk up the drive. Take in every detail. Look at the house, at its form, its design and its architecture. Look also at the gardens either side of the drive. After a time, you reach the front door of the house. You reach for the handle and open the door. Close the door behind you. You are now standing in a hallway. Look around at the hallway. Take in all the details. Look at the ceilings, the walls, the decorations and the colours. As you look round, you see a staircase. Look at the staircase. Look at its form and design, its bannisters (if any) and its shape. You start to walk up the staircase, you find yourself on the landing. In front if you are a series of doors. Decide which door you wish to head for and walk along the landing to the door you have chosen. Again take in the details of the landing, look at the other doors as you pass, their colours and their shape. When you reach your chosen door, open it, and walk inside. You will find yourself in a totally white room. There appears to be no windows. Everything is white. There are no features which you can take in, but as you look around, you see another door – you might have missed this door the first time, because it is also painted white. Reach for the handle and open the door. You find yourself in another room. Look around the room. Look at its contents, the furniture in it, the colour scheme. Take in every detail. You may wish to walk over to the window or windows. Look at their form. Look down to the gardens below. See where you are in relation to the house you walked up to. You can stay in that room as long as you wish. When you feel the time is right, you can decide to leave the room. Remember that you shut the door behind you, go back into the white anteroom, and then out on to the landing. Again take in all the details. They may have changed. Slowly walk back down the landing to the stairs. As you stand at the top of the stairs, look back at the landing, then slowly make your way down the staircase to the hallway below. Look around at the hallway. Look back at the staircase. Eventually, you make your way back to the door. Open it, walk through it and close the door behind you. You are outside again. You may, at this stage, wish to take a walk around the house in which you have just been, taking in all the views and sights, looking upwards to find the window at which you stood. Once this is done, walk slowly back down the drive, and before you reach the gate, turn back and look at the house. Is it the same house that you walked up to, or has it changed, even if only slightly. Open the gate, walk through the gate, and close it behind you. When you feel the time is right for you, leave behind the visualisation, have a stretch, let your breathing return to normal and open your eyes.

I have used this visualisation many times, and discovered that each of us visualises different things. With an understanding of

symbolism, you can then come to appreciate what is going on in the unconscious mind. Some people actively seek to recall places they have visited, or homes in which they would like to live. Many women, especially, think of places they have lived with loved ones, or even of thatched cottages in which they might like to live. I personally see a huge stately home, and interestingly when I walk up to the house, it seems to have a flat frontage, but when I leave, the windows are more rounded. Things obviously are softer to the eye, reflecting the fact that I am more relaxed and rounded in my mind. The hallway I find myself in is huge, with a crystal chandelier and an oak, winding, staircase. The room I go into after the white antechamber is a large study, with shelves of books and a big desk with a leather top. The window I see is a bowed window with a window seat made out of green leather running around it. As I look out of the window, I see manicured gardens and neatly trimmed hedges. Maybe I have delusions of grandeur, but perhaps you, when having thought about the symbolism involved, with the knowledge that you have gained, can see that there are a lot of symbols here which can tell you a great deal both about me and about my general state of mind. Working on the premise that the building is representative of me and my personal image, this meditation could well be telling me to think larger than I normally do, or underlining that I need to have a larger and better opinion of myself. Those people who have an interest in psychology could perhaps tell me even more!

When you write down as much of this guided imagery as you can remember, look at the symbols of the things you have seen. Think about symbolism rather than at the actual things – look beyond the obvious to the more obscure. You may find that you have seen things which have an immediate connection with your daily life, but do look at the smaller details, at the shapes and the forms, at the pictures and images you have created. Work out for yourself what all this is telling you. As with dreams, much of it may be personal to you, and may have no global symbolic meaning. However, this could be very revealing when you take a look at some of the symbols we have discussed.

AFTER A MEDITATION

When you have successfully meditated, try if you possibly can to keep the serenity and state of relaxation you have attained. You can, when practised in the art of meditation, actively seek to recall the image you used when in everyday life, and that in itself will help to bring about a state of calm and relaxation. I remember really clearly using my symbol of a rose when I worked in a large office. When I felt that I really was tense and likely to end up with a migraine unless I relaxed, I used to take myself off to the ladies room, and actively visualise my symbol for a couple of minutes. The process of doing this unwound me, and I also found that by running my wrists under cold water to feel action of the water on my body, also helped me to unwind.

Meditation is one of those things which some people take to easily and some people don't. Please try not to be hard on yourself if you find it a difficult task. You are an individual, you should never compare yourself to other people. Personally, I feel that meditation is a hugely rewarding experience, deep in symbolic meaning and useful as a tool to unwind and reach a state of physical and spiritual tranquility. You may well have a different viewpoint. All I can say is that, whatever viewpoint you may have, do give meditation a try. Even if you feel unhappy with the concept, it will at the very least help to relax.

*L ike many people, sometimes when I am in the middle of a
telephone call, or when I am waiting to be put through to someone,
or in the past when I was at a conference and finding the subject
matter a little boring, I pick up a pen or pencil and start to doodle on
a pad. Sometimes the shapes drawn are representative of nothing in
particular, but sometimes, in fact quite often, these doodles are symbols
from my own subconscious of things which, perhaps, I would prefer to
ignore, much the same as some dreams, which can give a clear
indication of problem areas.*

Looking at doodles, both our own and those of others, can be a
fascinating experience, and we can, once we understand the symbols
involved, learn an awful lot about what is going on under the surface.

During the course of this chapter, we are going to take a look at
some common doodles, and discuss their meaning as symbols.
Graphology, a science in its own right concerned with the character
analysis of handwriting, is the subject of another book within this
series, but doodles are symbols and signs. However, it is worthwhile
remembering that sometimes, as with dreams, doodles can be
personal things which link with events in our lives at present or in
the past. For example, it is commonly recognised in the field of
psychiatry that art therapy (the drawing of doodles and/or pictures)
can tell the doctor an awful lot about the problems, fears and needs
of the patient concerned. Patients are encouraged to draw symbolic
portraits of people, feelings and objects, not as they are, but as
images, shapes and colours. Art therapy is especially used in the
treatment of addiction, eating disorders and mental handicap, and is
often done in group sessions.

The position and form of doodles

As with graphology, when looking at doodles we have to consider where on the page these are placed, and how they are drawn. If you are tense or angry, you are likely to put a lot of pressure on your pen or pencil, resulting in a heavy doodle. People whose doodles are always on the heavy side are generally outgoing and self-assured types who know both what they want and where they are going. If, however, you are feeling relatively happy and light-hearted, a lighter stroke will, in all probability be used; light doodles also being common amongst those people who are not sure of themselves. Sensitive and imaginative people, these are the perfectionists amongst us, who subconsciously seek to do things in outline, thinking them through carefully, before committing themselves.

Large doodles in the middle of the page normally indicate the importance you place on yourself – this is how you see yourself. Bang in the middle of things, important and a focal point. This is the person who is likely to dress in bright colours, wear a lot of jewellery and feel the need to be noticed. These people are the extroverts amongst us, and even if the person themselves are considered shy, you can be sure that there is an extrovert there, just trying to get out. If, however, your doodle is in the margin or corner of a page, you are possibly a quieter person, reserved and retiring – someone who prefers to work unnoticed rather than making a statement about yourself. Those who draw small doodles are usually modest people, in speech, dress and behaviour, although likely to be very conscious about their appearance. Small doodles are usually those of people who take time to do things, and pay attention to detail. Often good in company, they also like to spend time alone. Doodles which start at the bottom of a page and go upwards normally indicate an ambitious person – heading for the top, whilst doodles which start in the middle or at the top and work downwards can indicate someone who is a little more introverted.

I am left handed. At one time, that in itself was considered a symbol of evil, and people who were left handed were actively made to write with their right hand. I personally know people who were forced to write right handed, and many of them became ambidextrous as a result of being rapped on the knuckles with a ruler by a teacher. That aside, as a result, my doodles usually start on the right and go left. Right-handed people may find their doodles going the other way. Where you start your doodles can, however, be relevant. If they begin on the left and head towards the right, this can be interpreted as intuitive doodles, whereas should they start on the right and work to the left, they are based upon logic. Maybe I'm just logical! Sometimes, especially when I feel puzzled over things, I will doodle a question mark, obviously symbolising decisions I have to make, and thoughts I have to work through. At others times, I will doodle an exclamation mark, symbolic of my feelings of achievement, but also quite a phallic symbol.

CONSTRUCTION, SIGNATURES AND COLOUR

Doodles which are rounded in form, generally speaking, show a person who will dress well and fashionably, someone who is quite emotional and impressionable. These are enthusiastic people who often lack aggression, but who hide a lot of emotion. Those people whose doodles are mostly angular or of a graphic nature, however, will be people who prefer order, dislike clutter and are less showy.

Doodles which are intricate, with lots of connected bits, involving several shapes and patterns, belong to people who like and need to express their personalities. Creative people often do this sort of doodle, as do those who are naturally active and energetic, and who seek new challenges at every opportunity. The problem sometimes lies in the fact that the person has a lot of challenges to meet, or conversely a lot of opportunities for change, and often is trying to achieve too many things at the same time, leading to a greater chance of failure. Repetitive doodles, especially of the same shape or design are symbolic of people with fixed opinions, lacking in originality but with an ordered and methodical mind. Should a letter of the alphabet be repeated to form a pattern, the person is possibly interested in education and likes repetitive work. Simple doodles, such as those detailing only a few shapes or marks normally are drawn by people who dislike change and new challenges, preferring the tried and tested route rather than anything involving a risk or a gamble.

One of the most common doodles I tend to do is filling in of capital letters which I write out, or sometimes find on another piece of paper by the telephone. Symbolically, this indicates that I like to lead rather than initiate new ideas, and that I like routine, prefer to work around a given guideline, follow orders and work with a team rather than alone. I'm basically a conformist – something which friends of mine can probably confirm! When I was a lot younger, I used to continually practise my signature, sometimes even changing the surname to that of a pop idol or someone I fancied. Signature writing is often symbolic of a need to underline the identity, and is very common amongst those who are newly married.

Colour of doodles also can be symbolic of hidden thoughts, unless, of course, you have to happen only a certain colour available at any one time! Blue is usually chosen by people with a friendly, outgoing attitude, whilst black is chosen by people who are more conventional, want to impress or who are efficient. Red is a sensual colour, and is chosen by people who want to make a statement, are confident, and like to be noticed. Green, on the other hand, is often chosen by people in a period of transition, learning about themselves, or who want to appear different from everybody else.

Looking at the symbolism

Taking a look at some of the more common doodles, we will see, from the information we have already learnt, that there are many common thoughts behind the symbols. Many of the doodles we

draw are shapes we have already come across and discussed, although it is worthwhile realising that there may be a personal significance, especially if the symbol is obviously job-related or related to a recent event or to someone close.

Triangular shapes

These are symbolic of organisation, and thus suggest that the person is a good organiser. This is someone who is thoughtful and capable, and who could go far in life. If there are a lot of sharp points, however, this is someone who can have a terrible temper when roused.

Square and oblong shapes

These are symbolic of feeling boxed in, or feeling generally down. However, they also symbolise a good business brain, especially if the boxes are then filled in to appear more solid and sturdy.

Aeroplanes

Aeroplanes are considered by most to be a phallic symbol, and are mostly doodles by adolescent boys who are concerned with sexual matters. **Lips** are also sexual symbols, but mostly drawn by women, whilst **breasts** will be drawn by young men.

Arrows

Arrows are obviously connected with aggression, as are **guns** and any form of **weaponry**. They can also be connected with ambition, with direction and determination. Also thought to be indicative of someone who is sexually demanding, a person who draws an arrow next to a **snail** is really someone to be watched, as snails are also symbolic of the sexual urge, as are **bullets**.

Boats

Boats are things in which to escape. Symbolic of the need to get away from people and relax, this symbol could indicate the need for a holiday, as could the doodle of **birds**, especially if the wings are drawn outspread. Should the boat be placed upon **wavy lines**, symbolic of the sea and of waves, there is a real wish to travel overseas, or even to have a holiday romance!

Boxes

These are basically square shapes, and as we have seen, representative of stability. They obviously also relate to the square and oblong-shaped doodles which we have already mentioned. They are symbolic of privacy, closed thinking, organised and methodical minds, as are any doodles which appear to be three dimensional, which also symbolise ambition. Boxes which are stacked one upon another symbolise someone who is especially methodical and logical, and as they can be seen to represent steps, also someone who perhaps is thinking about climbing up the social ladder, knowing that is is just a matter of time before they get to the top. It is interesting that boxes seem to be drawn mostly by men, although I also draw boxes as I am sure many women do, and it can be thought that the drawing of a closed box is symbolic of being self-centred, self-contained and private, with a need to conform but a possible wish to rebel. If the box is drawn closed and then tied with string, as you may tie up a parcel to send through the post, there may be a problem with relating to others, with feeling cut off, and an inability to be open and communicate problems. Should the box be drawn opened at one end, this symbolises the fact that you now feel able to let others into your space, and into your life, or conversely feel able to allow yourself a little more freedom.

Cars

These are a common doodle, coming from the box and square shape, and representing both stability and movement. If you doodle a big car, you could be merely thinking of moving up the social ladder, or just indulging in a flight of fancy.

Cobwebs

Cobwebs are symbolic of feeling trapped, just as the fly is trapped by the spider's web. Conversely, you could be wishing to trap someone in a web of your own! Similarly **spirals** indicate a feeling

of going round in circles and feeling trapped, and it is likely that these shapes will be drawn by people who are somewhat moody.

Dots

Dots are one of the basic symbols, as we have already found. Symbolic of new ideas, thought and creativity, they can also be considered to represent a state of stress and lack of focus.

Eyes

These again are a common symbol, and unless you are an optician in which case the doodle can be job related, eyes, especially if drawn repeatedly, symbolise the fact that you feel you are being watched all the time.

Faces

These are a very common doodle. Said by psychiatrists to be drawn mostly by teenage girls, the face can reflect the restriction of the parents, but also the idle fantasies involved in early love affairs. Conversely, especially if drawn by older adults, it can indicate a person who is obsessed with appearance, of themselves, their partners and their families. These are the people who like the company of others, and often they are drawn by people who are creative in the writing sense. Cartoon faces, however, seem to be mostly drawn by men, and are symbolic of the need to be noticed as different from the rest. Those people who doodle ugly or sinister looking faces may be going through a bad patch, have problems with their nerves and/or feel isolated. It is worthwhile pointing out that many people, at certain times in their lives, can doodle this sort of image, and it is something which passes. Most faces are drawn from the front, rather than in profile, indicating an observant, lively person with a positive attitude.

Flowers

Flowers are romantic symbols. Mostly drawn by women, roses especially are a common doodle, symbolic of the need to feel loved and the desire to be cherished, which might not be otherwise expressed.

Those with strong maternal and protective instincts, especially towards children and animals, seem more drawn to doodle flowers.

Hearts

These are concerned with love, romance and the need for security. These doodles are often alongside doodles of houses and stars. As we have already seen, hearts when pierced by arrows are a distinct phallic symbol, even if not consciously recognised as such.

Houses

Houses relate to security, and again stem from the box shape or square. This is a very common doodle. If a huge house is drawn, there is a need for space or maybe just delusions of grandeur! Most house doodles are drawn by women, and if the doors and windows are open, this indicates that a welcome is assured, as is the case if smoke if drawn coming from a chimney. Should there be no windows, this is a sign of unhappiness. Drawing a **cat** by the door suggests security, home and family, but can also symbolise the need to get away, be independent and free – it depends whether you feel that the cat is entering the house, or leaving it.

Keys

Keys are, as we have discussed, things which open doors leading to new places. As such, drawing a key could symbolise the need for a new beginning or the need to escape from a situation or person causing concern and frustration. This is the case especially if the key is placed near to a doodle of a labyrinth or maze from which you either wish to escape or in which you feel safe.

Stars

These are mostly drawn by women. Symbolic of romance, idealism and the hope of a happy relationship, if drawn by men they can be symbolic of the need for recognition, especially if that person has showbiz connections. As with the general symbolism behind stars, a lot of hope is being expressed in realising plans for the future.

Trees

Trees are symbolic of stability, and can also have a huge phallic significance. When drawn by children, trees are thought to symbolise someone interesting in learning. If drawn without leaves, this symbolises a feeling of barrenness and isolation, whilst a tree which is shown swaying in the wind and losing its leaves symbolises the feeling of being blown about in all directions and feeling insecure, particularly in a relationship.

Snakes

Considered to be representative of wisdom by many, snakes can also be symbolic of the feeling that something or someone cannot be trusted, and is likely to slip away. Snakes are another phallic symbol, representing the need for a physical relationship, as can doodles of **lizards** or **fish**.

This is not a full list of all the differing types of doodles people will draw. It is just a selection, concentrating on symbols which we may have encountered before in a slightly different light.

Looking back, and towards the future

In this book we have covered a lot of different signs and symbols, trying to concentrate our efforts on the geometric and abstract shapes and the object and picture symbols. There are obviously limitless other symbols and signs which could have been discussed, but I have tried to concentrate on the more basic symbols, giving a platform from which to move forwards, leading to further study, should you wish to do so.

As with any form of symbolism, the end meaning can often be a personal thing, totally unrelated to anything which others have suggested. As many dreams relate directly to the personal circumstances of the dreamer, the same will also apply with the meaning of certain symbols. I have tried to give as many as possible of the accepted symbolic meanings of the various points discussed. We have seen how certain symbols seem to have a universal meaning, irrespective of country, religious leanings or academic theory. This is particularly true of the geometric or graphic symbols. To students of psychiatry, and especially to students of Freud, most symbols will relate to things of a sexual nature. As a result, many of the signs and symbols we have covered could seem to be phallic in meaning, even if this has not been mentioned in the text. Again, this serves to underline that symbolism can be a very complex and varied topic, and we have only skimmed the surface in this book.

I hope that you will now understand the complexities of symbolism and wish to learn more. If you are particularly interested in dream symbolism, which I have been unable to cover here, you might wish to research from a psychological viewpoint, rather than by reference to books which merely list various topics and give standardised meanings, interesting though these may be. However, I leave this to you to determine the best course for yourself. Similarly, if you are interested in learning more about meditation and visualisation techniques, and wish to use symbolism in your studies, you may wish to seek out specific books on those subjects and go on to form your own symbolism from your own personal endeavours. Various book exist on symbolism generally, and some of these are listed in the Further Reading section at the end of this book. Again, this is not exhaustive, but serves merely as a guide.

At the end of the day, it is important that you feel comfortable with any symbol you actively use on a day-to-day basis, and this is something only you can find for yourself by practice. Only by actively seeking out what is right for you can you ever hope to grow in awareness. By the same token, only by truly understanding ourselves, our conscious and unconscious minds, can we ever be expected to understand other people. My hope is that through this book you might have learnt a little more about yourself from considering the symbols you use, see and draw on a day-to-day basis.

FURTHER READING

Chetwynd, Tom, *Dictionary for Dreamers*, Thorsons.

Chetwynd, Tom, *Dictionary of Symbols*, Thorsons.

Cirlot, J E, *A Dictionary of Symbols*, Routledge, 1988.

Cooper, J C, *An Illustrated Encyclopaedia of Traditional Symbols*, Thames and Hudson, 1978.

Cooper, J C, *Dictionary of Symbolic and Mythical Animals*, Thorsons, 1992.

Koch, R, *The Book of Signs*, London, 1930.

Lehner, *Symbols, Signs and Signets*, Cleveland, 1950.

Pavitt, W, *The Book of Talismans, Amulets, and Zodiacal Gems*, Wiltshire Book Co.

Pennick, N, *The Secret Lore of Runes and Other Ancient Alphabets*, Rider, 1991.

de Vries, A, *Dictionary of Symbols and Images*, Amsterdam, 1974.

OTHER TITLES IN THIS SERIES

Astral Projection 0 340 67418 0   £5.99   Is it possible for the soul to leave the body at will? In this book the traditional techniques used to achieve astral projection are described in a simple, practical way, and Out of the Body and Near Death Experiences are also explored.

Chakras 0 340 62082 X   £5.99   The body's energy centres, the chakras, can act as gateways to healing and increased self-knowledge. This book shows you how to work with chakras in safety and with confidence.

Chinese Horoscopes 0 340 64804 X   £5.99   In the Chinese system of horoscopes, the year of birth is all-important. *Chinese Horoscopes for beginners* tells you how to determine your own Chinese horoscope, what personality traits you are likely to have, and how your fortunes may fluctuate in years to come.

Dowsing 0 340 60882 X   £5.99   People all over the world have used dowsing since the earliest times. This book shows how to start dowsing – what to use, what to dowse, and what to expect when subtle energies are detected.

Dream Interpretation 0 340 60150 7   £5.99   This fascinating introduction to the art and science of dream interpretation explains how to unravel the meaning behind dream images to interpret your own and other people's dreams.

Feng Shui 0 340 62079 X   £5.99   This beginner's guide to the ancient art of luck management will show you how to increase your good fortune and well-being by harmonising your environment with the natural energies of the earth.

Gems and Crystals 0 340 60883 8   £5.99   For centuries gems and crystals have been used as an aid to healing and meditation. This guide tells you all you need to know about choosing, keeping and using stones to increase your personal awareness and improve your well-being.

The Goddess 0 340 68390 2   £5.99   This book traces the development, demise and rebirth of the Goddess, looking at the worship of Her and retelling myths from all over the world.

Graphology 0 340 60625 8   £5.99   Graphology, the science of interpreting handwriting to reveal personality, is now widely accepted and used throughout the world. This introduction will enable you to make a comprehensive analysis of your own and other people's handwriting to reveal the hidden self.

Herbs for Magic and Ritual 0 340 67415 6   £4.99   This book looks at the well-known herbs and the stories attached to them. There is information on the use of herbs in essential oils and incense, and on their healing and magical qualities.

I Ching 0 340 62080 3   £5.99   The roots of *I Ching* or the *Book of Changes* lie in the time of the feudal mandarin lords of China, but its traditional wisdom is still relevant today. Using the original poetry in its translated form, this introduction traces its history, survival and modern-day applications.

Interpreting Signs and Symbols 0 340 68827 0   £5.99   The history of signs and symbols is traced in this book from their roots to the modern age. It also examines the way psychiatry uses symbolism, and the significance of doodles.